Ever present

Never twice the same

Ever changing

Never less than whole

ROBERT IRWIN

IVP
7.15

CHECK ALL THAT APPLY
Finding Wholeness as a Multiracial Person

SUNDEE TUCKER FRAZIER

InterVarsity Press
Downers Grove, Illinois

InterVarsity Press
P.O. Box 1400, Downers Grove, IL 60515-1426
World Wide Web: www.ivpress.com
E-mail: mail@ivpress.com

InterVarsity Press® is the book-publishing division of InterVarsity Christian Fellowship/USA®, a
student movement active on campus at hundreds of universities, colleges and schools of nursing in
the United States of America, and a member movement of the International Fellowship of Evangelical
Students. For information about local and regional activities, write Public Relations Dept.,
InterVarsity Christian Fellowship/USA, 6400 Schroeder Rd., P.O. Box 7895, Madison, WI
53707-7895, or visit the IVCF website at <www.ivcf.org>.

Scripture quotations, unless otherwise noted, are from the New Revised Standard Version of the Bible,
copyright 1989 by the Division of Christian Education of the National Council of the Churches of
Christ in the U.S.A. Used by permission. All rights reserved.

Poems by Lori Dinkins, Melissa Camacho, Nathan Baird, Isaac Tucker and Alexis Spencer-Byers
used by permission of the authors.

Song lyrics by Matt Frazier used by permission of the author.

Cover photograph: 2100 Productions

ISBN 0-8308-2247-X

Printed in the United States of America ∞

Library of Congress Cataloging-in-Publication Data has been requested.

23 22 21 20 19 18 17 16 15 14 13 12 11 10 9 8 7 6 5 4 3 2 1

20 19 18 17 16 15 14 13 12 11 10 09 08 07 06 05 04 03 02

To my brother, Isaac,
because you understand.

Contents

Introduction _____ 9

PART 1: Identity Issues

1 Don't Make Me Choose_____ 19
2 Not Always As We Appear _____ 31
3 How Can I Be Many in One? _____ 49
4 Our Core Identity_____ 69

PART 2: Relating to Others

5 Temptations We Face_____ 82
6 All in the Family_____ 95
7 As if Dating and Marriage Weren't Complicated Enough_____ 114

PART 3: Walking in Purpose and Wholeness

8 Made Multiracial for a Reason_____ 130
9 Where Can We Find Wholeness? _____ 145

Epilogue _____ 161
Glossary of Terms _____ 165
Appendix 1: Race, Ethnicity, Culture—What's the Difference?_____ 167
Appendix 2: We're Not Alone: Historical Examples
    of Multiracial People_____ 174
Appendix 3: Resources _____ 186
Bibliography_____ 198

Introduction

I admit it: I'm confusing. I belong to more than one race. Involuntarily at first, now gladly, I am biracial. Though I'm grateful for my ethnic mix, it's a strange existence being in the middle, on the margins.

I floated through my first seventeen years of life, not paying much attention to my race. I was black and white and proud of it. My peers accepted me well enough, but I considered myself a loner, really. Attending predominantly white schools, I knew instinctively to guard myself. As far as I was concerned, my little brother was the only other person on the planet who understood.

In college I was initiated into racial hostility and difference, and I bumped and bounced back and forth between my segregated groups of friends, trying to figure out where I belonged. As I grew increasingly aware of my one people's racism toward my other people, it became harder to be in all-white groups without burning over the ignorance, disinterest and contentment with the status quo that I sensed—frighteningly, even in myself at times. It was painful to know white people who liked *me* but who, if the truth were told, were scared of black people and would never be alone in a group of them; they would never voluntarily be in the minority. I was in the minority *wherever* I went.

Tension over racial belonging mounted through my twenties until one night, at age twenty-nine, I had it out with God—the One I had come to understand and believe was ultimately responsible for my racially mixed creation.

It was an annual gathering of my employer's black staff. We were a small group of thirty or so. I was no longer new in this setting. Other rookies had joined the ranks, and now I sat comfortably above initiate but certainly well below veteran level. I no longer felt like an outsider looking in. It felt good. Over four days we talked, planned, shared vision, ate and laughed together.

Our focus was accepting one another, including our diverse backgrounds and the various roles we played in our organization. The last night I had the opportunity to read a poem that spoke of my growing acceptance of myself as a biracial person. It had been one of my first attempts, written just a couple of months earlier. It had come to me in a flash—so fluidly, in fact, that I attributed its existence to God's inspiration.

After I read, a coworker led an affirmation time in which each person in the room was to choose someone else and say something admirable about him or her to the whole group. A young staff member, a rookie, affirmed me by saying, "It's really great to see a white woman be so into black culture."

My heart dropped. I stood horrified as awkward silence filled the room. The whole week he had thought I was white, even though it was a meeting for black people. The comfort I had worked years to achieve vanished in an instant. Had he not understood the poem I had read just minutes earlier? I thought its message was pretty clear: *"I'm black too!"*

Fortunately, nearly everyone else in the room knew my background, and they set the brother straight. Unfortunately, the damage was done. I swallowed my emotions the rest of the evening, until a heavy prayer time for our director and his wife brought tears among us all. Only I cried for myself.

As soon as the session was over, I bolted. I didn't want anyone to see me or know how I truly felt. But God wouldn't let me get away that easily. In the lobby I encountered someone who insightfully asked if I had felt hurt earlier. I couldn't hold back the tears. He loaned me his handkerchief and some comforting words, and I took off again. I was angry and hurt, and I was going to tell God off because he had made me invisible to my own people.[1]

As I left the building, a figure from behind caught my eye. My heart skipped a beat. It was the offending brother, the one who had spoken what he didn't know. He saw my tears. His eyes widened as he realized that his words had opened a major wound in my life. "Did I hurt you by what I said?" he asked.

I cried more. I was extremely embarrassed *(God, why are you doing this to me?)*, but I answered truthfully.

The young man (younger than me) looked me in the eye and asked my forgiveness for not having listened when I read my poem. Then he said, "You are a black sister. I'm sorry I didn't recognize that before. But ultimately what matters when people see you is that they see Jesus, not whether they see black or white."

I knew he was right and his words were important. I was grateful, but I still needed to do some fighting with God.

I cried longer and harder that night than I ever had about my biracial existence and particularly how I look. Clearly this one man's oblivious comment was not the sole cause of the pain I felt. It was just the final torque that had loosened the plug of my backlogged feelings. I was angry at God for how he had made me, the skin tone he had given me, my hair (I could see its shape in my shadow, so flat and limp)—and I told him so. I felt forever excluded from being "in" with my darker brothers and sisters, and doomed to a life of defending my racial makeup and my existence before both whites and blacks. I sat on a log and cried.

I told God I was angry with my parents. Had they thought about what it would be like for me before they did what they did? Most likely not: I was conceived out of wedlock. I cried some more. Did God get it? Was he understanding me? Did he *care?*

Suddenly, effortlessly, I heard the lines of my own poem being whis-

---

[1]Please understand that when I refer to God as a "he" it is not because I think God is a man or masculine only. Our language is limited and insufficient for describing God. However, we do our best.

pered into my ear, scrolling across the screen of my mind and the star-flooded sky:

Zebra
Oreo
Octoroon

Mulatto
Multiracial
Cablinasian?

"What *are* you?"

What are *you?*
I am AmericanAfricanScottishDutchDanishSwedeIndigenousPerson
Human being!
Child of God!
child of God
Knit perfectly in my mother's womb
Exactly as I was meant to be
I am me
Sundee

I had titled the poem "Confusing, but Not Confused"—a title for myself, really (although to be honest, sometimes I still feel confused). It is about resisting people's attempts to label those who don't make sense to them. It is about refusing others' definitions and choosing self- and God-definition.

When I have relapses of confusion, the poem reminds me of the truth. God knew I needed to hear the truth right then. In fact, I believe he had me write the poem because he knew I'd need it at that exact moment. My anger and hurt subsided, and I thanked God for reminding me of who I was—that I was his child, especially, created perfectly in my mother's womb exactly as I was meant to be.

A Growing Need

Being multiracial in a racially splintered world can be grueling. We want and need help. We are striving to reconcile and maintain multiple racial, ethnic and cultural identities within our one person.

Frequently confronted with others' desire or need for us to identify ourselves, we wonder who we really are, wrestle with our appearance, fight with our family background. We ask, *Who will I marry?* or *What will my kids do, being even more mixed than I?* We face multitudes of temptations—to think more highly of ourselves than we ought, or not to value ourselves highly enough.

In this book I address all of these topics. I believe multiracial people have much in common regardless of racial mixture. We have been created as a group and as individuals for a significant destiny. And we *can* live as whole people—I hope this book will encourage your confidence about that.

As I've written, I have kept images of other multiracial people— especially children, our future—before my eyes. I have kept in my ears the excited thank-yous I've heard when I mentioned I was writing such a book. I have remembered the words of my younger friend Stacy, when I asked her what she did and didn't like about being biracial: "I don't like that there aren't many resources out there for a biracial identity." Stacy is in heaven now, and I trust that she is enjoying being fully herself in a way she never could have experienced in this life.

Fortunately for those of us who are striving to live as whole people, who embrace *both* or *all* (often in protest of the tyranny of racism in America and the world), we are increasingly not alone. Many of us have been seeking out answers by ourselves. Now we are beginning to find one another, and the result of our collaboration is a small but growing canon—books, documentaries, web sites, poetry, research, models of multiracial and multiethnic identity. Future generations will have places to turn for help.

And future generations there will be. The number of interracial marriages in the United States grew from a mere 310,000 in 1970 to over 1.3 million in 1994 (and this doesn't include interethnic marriages). In 1990 the Census Bureau reported that one in twenty-five married couples was interracial. Californian interracial marriages numbered one in ten. I have seen figures putting the number of multiracial children at between two and four million. The 2000 census, which for the first time allowed respondents to "check all that apply," reported that nearly seven million people (2.4 percent of the American population) had done just that.

Some question how much multiracial people really have in common given the variety of mixes, backgrounds and experiences among us. Does a multiracial community in fact exist? The burgeoning number of resources and the fact that there clearly has been an audience for them is evidence to me that we have a common experience regardless of our mixture. So is the proliferation of interracial family support groups and of campus groups formed by and for multiracial students of all backgrounds.

It may be that the most we have in common is our experience of being "both" and yet "neither" (or "all" and yet "none"). We refuse to cut off parts of ourselves to appease others. If so, this refusal has so profoundly shaped our views of the world and ourselves that we want to talk about it. We want to make sense of it. We want it to work out for good. We want it to be recognized.

Names are important because they point to one's nature. We have decided that our nature is not this *or* that but this *and* that. Not surprisingly, we want a name that reflects dualism and not dichotomy. Naming something or someone is a way of asserting one's ownership or authority over it, him or her. Since the civil rights movement, the majority no longer has the right to name a minority group—we name ourselves. Many of us are naming ourselves "biracial" or "multiracial" because in our opinion these terms best reflect our nature and experience.

Even though this book is about multiracial and multiethnic wholeness, I don't assume that every multiracial person who reads it has chosen or will choose a multiracial identity. Some feel most comfortable claiming a single-race identity because of how they've been raised, how they look or just because it "fits." Some feel politically convicted that retaining a single-race identity is the right thing to do. Perhaps this book will solidify your choices; perhaps it will touch things in you that you didn't know were there.

Though I desire this book to be applicable to monoracial people who are bicultural due to adoption, immigration or living in a racially integrated environment, it will undoubtedly fall short. However, whether there is a mixture of two races in your "blood" or only in your heart, most likely you will find issues and principles that apply to your situation.

One last disclaimer: As an American, I write from an American point of view. Most of the stories and racial dynamics that I discuss are taken from my experience in the United States. If you are from another country, I hope that much of the material will translate. The United States has a peculiar racial history, but forms of ethnic elitism prevail in most societies, undoubtedly making life challenging for dual-heritage citizens anywhere.

The book is organized around three central themes: identity, relationships and purpose. The issue of finding wholeness permeates it all. Part one, "Identity Issues," deals with the constant pressure we face to choose a race, how our looks affect our experience, how we can live out an identity that integrates a multiethnic heritage, how we find the core of our personhood. Part two, "Relating to Others," addresses relationships—with God, our families and "that special someone." Part three, "Walking in Purpose and Wholeness," explores the reasons for our creation, the special roles we can play in this increasingly multicultural world and the source of our wholeness.

Throughout, I tell the stories and share the thoughts of various mixed-race people I have encountered. Sometimes they are named and sometimes not; the examples vary in length and depth. My personal process of finding wholeness is woven throughout the book, not chronologically (it's been much too complicated for that) but according to chapter topics. I tell stories because I believe we can learn from each other how to be wholly multiracial. We also need the companionship, a reminder that we are not alone on this journey.

Our Greatest Resource

Ultimately, for *all* of us, regardless of our racial identity, the greatest resource for wholeness is our Creator. "O the depth of the riches and wisdom and knowledge of God!" (Rom 11:33). The One who made everything, including us, knows all there is to know and can therefore provide the most satisfying answers. The Creator makes sense of our existence.

I realize that not all of those reading this book come from the same faith perspective that I embrace. But I believe that regardless of spiritual background, anyone interested in the multiracial experience will find something helpful in these pages.

My perspective is that God is real and personal, and he knows each of us intimately because we are his creation. The Bible says it was God who formed our inward parts; he handcrafted us in our mother's womb. This is powerful news for any of us who have felt like a mistake or wondered if we should have been born one race or the other, one culture or the other.

As a Christian, I believe that Jesus was God revealing himself to humankind. And Jesus cared about the situation of multiracial people during his time! First, he too was multiracial (we'll look at his genealogy later). Second, Jesus strategically and single-handedly redefined the historical perception of Samaritans, a mixed-race group despised by most Jews of that era.

To this day, when you hear the word *Samaritan* you think "good," right? Well, the Samaritans were multiracial (Jewish and Assyrian), and they were called everything *but* good before Jesus came along. But Jesus cared about Samaritans, and he changed their reputation forever with his story about a Samaritan who went out of his way to care for a man beaten nearly to the point of death. Now we've got Good Samaritan hospitals all over the place—a constant reminder that Jesus cared about mixed-race people.

I've found that Jesus, like me, was a "both/and" person. One of the aspects of Jesus that mystifies us all, and causes many to reject him, is that he claimed to be both a human being and God. While on earth he lived out this both/and existence perfectly. People didn't get him any more than they get multiracialness. They excoriated him for making such a claim, but he refused to be anything less than who he was.

There is a difference between Jesus and us, of course. We are only human. All of our races are 100 percent bona fide *Homo sapiens,* and thus equal in the eyes of God. Humanity is not equal to God, making Jesus' incarnation a supernatural event, incomprehensible to even the sharpest mind. But black humanity *is* equal to white humanity, making my birth, frankly, not that hard to grasp (though all births are still miracles of divine gift).

The tension surrounding my both/and existence has to do with human-made constructs, which thrive on hierarchies that God doesn't endorse and in fact is working to abolish. It's a problem for us to be who we are only when all races are not considered equal or when others insist on defining us exclusively based on what they see or who they want us to be.

Our challenge is to resist society's limiting and inflexible racial categories and be who we truly are, whether people like it or not. "The biracial and bicultural person strives for a totalness, a sense of wholeness that is more than the sum of the parts of a person's heritages" (Root, *Racially Mixed People*, p. 317).[2] When I first read this, my entire being agreed with a resounding *Yes! This is what I want—multiracial and multiethnic wholeness.*

I'm not there yet, but I'm moving toward it—a place where I am completely myself no matter what racial or ethnic setting I'm in, a place where others' impressions of me don't have more power than my knowledge of myself.

One day my husband, Matt, who is white, and I had breakfast with our pastors, Fred and Juanita Davis, who are black. Pastor Fred spoke words into my heart that I will never forget. I cried as I listened because I so longed for them to be fulfilled. He said, "My prayer for you is that you will become as comfortable with being who you are as Matt is being who he is and I am being who I am."

Now his prayer for me is my prayer for you. May this book help you to be more comfortable with who you are, with who God has made you perfectly to be.

A Note About Labels

I have tried my best to use terms that are popularly accepted and used by the majority of people within an ethnic group. Thus I use both *African American* and *black*—particularly because *black* is more inclusive

---

[2]See the bibliography for full publication information.

of the entire African Diaspora. I use both *Latino* and *Hispanic,* even though I recognize that some don't like the latter because of its association with the historic oppressor. I use *American Indian, Native American* and *First Nations,* though my understanding is that indigenous people identify first with their specific tribe. I refer to a person's specific Asian country of origin whenever possible; otherwise I use the inclusive *Asian American* or *Asian.* Please forgive me if I use a term that offends you or betrays my ignorance. In dealing with race, I am bound to step on toes along the way. Please see the glossary for definitions of other terms.

1

Don't Make Me Choose

It was so hot, muggy and smoggy you couldn't see the mountain range just a few miles to the north. A typical summer day in Pasadena, California, circa 1988. I was nineteen years old and participating in an eight-week urban service project. I was ready to end poverty and bring justice to the inner city. But first we had to talk about race—something I didn't particularly enjoy doing because of the inevitable pain involved for me as a person of *two* races.

Of course, long before this fateful day I had filled out dozens of forms that forced me to check a little racial box. I never had a problem with it. I knew one of my parents was black and one was white. What did that make me? Sundee, I guess. But on forms I always chose "black" because somewhere along the way I had heard that you were automatically what your father was.[1]

---

[1] There's an old saying that black blood is more powerful than the blood of Jesus: one drop makes you black. This satirical saying stemmed from U.S. laws that stated that as little as 1/16 "Negro" ancestry made a person black, and thus subject to slavery, Jim Crow, or whatever was the discrimination du jour. Though these laws are no longer

Now, in the basement of a church in Pasadena, during an orientation with twenty other racially diverse interns, I would be forced to choose in a way I had never before faced.

Two men were there to train us in racial awareness and sensitivity. First they asked us to describe them—to say what we noticed about who they were. "One of you wears glasses." "One of you is bald." "One of you is taller than the other." "You're both men." I thought we had done a pretty good and thorough job, until they pointed out that none of us had mentioned that one was black and one was white.

Oh no, I thought, like someone whose blind date has just turned sour. At home we had always skirted subjects that might lead to conflict, including race. My internal defense mechanisms began to turn, and I steeled myself for turmoil.

A series of exercises put me a little more at ease. *(This isn't so bad,* I was soon assuring myself. *No one has screamed at anyone else or cried or used their chair as an assault weapon.)* I had just allowed myself to believe I might actually escape this basement-turned-torture-chamber without any gaping psychic or emotional wounds, when it was suddenly time to get with our "own people" so we could talk openly about our feelings. Ironically, the activity that everyone else perceived as the easiest and most comfortable undid me.

The various human colors and features separated into four corners. I stood paralyzed and alone in the middle. I was the one intern who needed to go to two groups. But I was only one person. All my body heat relocated to my face and armpits. *Don't cry, don't cry,* I pleaded with myself, trying to suppress my panic. Nothing remotely like this had ever happened to me.

"What's wrong?" one of the facilitators asked. Forty-some eyes suddenly fixed on me.

Great, I thought, *I'm now on display in the racial freak show hall of horrors: "Come see 'The Tragic Mulatto'!"* I had a feeling the facilitator knew my predicament. He seemed a little too eager to see how this

---

around, their effects on perceptions and attitudes, and the racism that spawned them, are alive and well.

would all come down. It surely was great grist for the racially charged mill he and his partner were trying to get churning.

I stared at him with urgent eyes. "Where am *I* supposed to go?" I asked.

"You have to choose."

The words landed like an ax—splitting me down the middle. I was being told to identify with one racial group over another in front of my peers. This was not the private choosing of an application form but a very public choosing that would have immediate social ramifications. *Welcome to the real world.*

I don't remember if the facilitator asked for group input, but the black students registered their votes. "If she was raised around white people and feels more comfortable with that then she should go with them," one of them said. "Nah, come with us, girl—you're one of us," said another. Suddenly I had become a grand case study of "those poor mixed children."

My mind spun in confusion and fear of making the wrong choice. I *had* grown up in mostly white settings, but I had also always been around both the white and black sides of my family. With them I never had to choose a side—we were all on the same side. I had no desire to reject either or be rejected by either.

I have a right to choose black, I thought to myself. My self thought back, *But what if they reject you?* Seconds felt like hours as I reasoned with my fears: *But I'm black, too, even if my experiences and phenotype are somewhat different.* I wanted my choice to state clearly, *I'm proud to be black,* but more than anything I wanted to scream, "Why are you making me choose? *Why?*"

I knew in my gut that it wasn't really an option for me to go with the white group. That choice would resonate in the room's collective subconscious as "uppity." I argued with myself (and with our country's messed-up racial paradigm), *But aren't I as much white as I am black?* My self argued back, *If you go with the whites, the blacks will not see you as one of them, and the whites will see you as one of the "safe" black people, if they even think of you as black at all. Everyone will probably think you are deluded and confused.*

If I deliberated much longer, it would become clear to all that I was very much confused.

In the end, my decision could not be simple because the development of race relations in the United States is not simple. I felt fearful and ashamed because the story of race in America is full of fear and shame. Our country's history of white hegemony, racial "passing" and the rule of hypodescent (assigning racially mixed people to their supposedly inferior and subordinate group) made going with the white students seem wrong. Plus I wanted the group to know I was black and proud of it. So I went with the black students.

But the fact remains that the situation was less than ideal for me as a biracial person.

My choice was affected by history but also by fear. I feared being myself. I feared rejection. I feared who I am. Ultimately I don't think my fears were irrational. They were based on a reality in this world, and particularly in this country: race still matters. If you are biracial or bicultural, you are automatically placed between factions that by and large don't trust one another. This is a fearful position because you're caught between warring parties and because everyone has an opinion about which side you should be on.

That day in a Pasadena church basement, I sat with my black peers and enjoyed a partial sense of belonging. I laughed when others laughed, even if I didn't totally get it. I mostly understood what everyone was talking about, though I hadn't always had the same experiences. I was accepted as a part of the group, but I also had to face the lonely truth that this "racial awareness and sensitivity training" had completely overlooked my racial reality.

Hurt by the Fences

The situations in which biracial people find themselves forced to choose are not always as dramatic as my experience in Pasadena. Yet the pressure we feel to choose is real and constant for one primary reason: *we live in a segregated society maintained by fear, apathy, arrogance and distrust of the "other."* For all the emphasis on celebrating diversity, historical and current racism and the resulting hurt and inequity have left us with a legacy of social and economic segregation.

As multiracial people, we are pressed by past and present strife and separation of the races to choose an allegiance. We know as well as anyone that there is still a humanly constructed, usually invisible, fence that keeps people on their own sides. The fence stakes poke us often as we climb back and forth, seeking to enjoy our full ethnic inheritance.

At least we *can* climb back and forth. Racist adherence to "ethnic purity" historically gave us no choice. At one time rejected by our ethnically "pure" predecessors wanting to keep their race "unsullied," those of us who claim to be multiracial are now being eyed to see what our identity choices mean for our politics, our commitment to justice or our regard for ethnic cohesiveness. Will we be loyal? Will we guard family secrets?

Forms collecting demographic data are one representation of this country's racial rigidity and a constant reminder that a race-based problem exists for which no satisfactory solution has been found. These forms force us regularly to choose one of our races over the other(s), or to pick the ambiguous catchall "Other."

Though information-gathering methods are gradually changing, for decades we were told to "select only one," and often we still are. The choices of many multiracial people fluctuate. "If anyone tracked my responses, they'd think I was schizophrenic," said a biracial friend of mine. "[Choosing one] is a very unpleasant feeling for me because part of me is being taken away. Or you can say 'other' and people don't know who you are. More and more I'm going to pick 'other' but it leaves me really unsatisfied. . . . It's a pinprick that reminds me the world's not ready for me yet."

To most people those little boxes don't seem like a big deal, but for those of us who acknowledge a multiracial background, they symbolize society's pressure that we just keep it simple and pick one already.

Though box checking can be quite frustrating (and even devaluing when I'm not allowed to identify my full ethnic background), it means little to the social realities of my day-to-day life. Much more difficult and damaging is how others evaluate me on the basis of what they see (or think they see). That's truly how we get categorized. Who I sit with at lunch, what clubs I join or what music I like can easily become the object of critique, commentary and castigation. Because everyone for the most part hangs out with others of the same race, we who are *both* end up going back and forth, or sticking primarily with one or the other.[2]

During a minority student orientation at University of California at Berkeley's law school, Lisa Feldstein, a black-Jewish biracial woman, asked members of a nonwhite panel how they interacted with white students. No one would say anything. Finally a black student panelist said, "Things around here get pretty tense; you'd best stick with your own kind."

"I didn't really know what to think," Lisa said later. She wondered facetiously who was her "own kind."

The next week the same black student came up to her and said, "You never hang out in the Law Students of African Descent Lounge."

She responded, "I'm not sure I feel particularly welcome there."

He said, "Let me give you the combination. Give me something to write it down on."

"I'll remember."

He replied, "No, I don't want any white people to hear."

Lisa refused the combination. He said he was just joking.

But she didn't think it was funny. She told him her father was white. He said he was sorry and walked away (Funderburg, pp. 129-30).

The young man's suspicion of whites is historically well founded and understandable. However, for Lisa it was a painful reminder that the fences remain. Her two sides war on.

The Case for Choosing

There are various reasons people want us to choose a race. Considering the motives and fears behind these reasons can help us to define our position while increasing our insight into the issues involved, our com-

---

[2]Christians have done no better in helping multiracial people in this regard. Truly multiethnic, diverse churches are almost nonexistent. So we are forced to choose again.

mitment to truth and justice, and our compassion for those who don't understand a multiracial choice.

Danger of disappearing. Some argue that biracial people should be raised with a monoracial identity to keep cultures intact. Ethnic minority group members, in particular, fear that as more people intermarry and more multiracial children are born, ethnic pride and loyalty will decline. Traditions and languages will not be passed on. Whole ethnic groups may eventually disappear if multiracial children are allowed to have multiple allegiances. When a person is part white, a multiracial identity is often seen as distancing oneself from the ethnic minority group to which he or she belongs (even though that is not necessarily the person's intent). Regardless of our mixture, we are perceived as "watering down" ethnic groups.[3]

Mixed-race people make this argument as well. In the article "Mulatto Millennium," Danzy Senna says that she was simply "a black girl" before multiracial people started making a fuss. She tried identifying herself as mixed but found that when she did others disregarded her black heritage (she says she looks more Jewish than black). People would make racist comments in her presence. When she would remind them that her father was black, they would say, "But you're different."

She writes, "There was danger in this muddy middle stance. A danger of disappearing. Of being swallowed whole by the great white whale. I had seen the arctic belly of the beast and didn't plan on returning" (O'Hearn, p. 18).

While some might ignore our ethnic heritage if we maintain a multiracial identity, causing us to "disappear," their opinions don't define reality. I *am* black whether or not others think I am. And their ignorance or prejudice won't keep me from being black.

Interracial mixing has existed in the United States since the earliest arrivals of nonindigenous people. Some would say this mixing

---

[3]Unfortunately, some Christians to this day oppose interracial marriage using the argument that God intends ethnic groups to remain intact and distinct from one another. Mixed marriages, they say, break down barriers God has established. See appendix one for my response.

has caused ethnic groups to disappear. Another perspective is that they are being re-created.[4]

Ethnic groups are not, nor have they ever been, static or monolithic. The fact that many people of Asian heritage in the United States now choose the title "Asian American" (or more specifically the country of their ancestors plus American) is evidence that group identity and culture are constantly in process. East and West are meeting, clashing and ultimately being synthesized within bicultural individuals of Asian descent in America.

African American culture, as it exists today, is a mix of influences—African, European and Native American. This re-created and quite diverse ethnic group has significantly affected our country's practice of civil rights and openness to spiritual matters. African Americans have created new music, art and celebrations that are fundamental to the overall landscape and culture of the United States.

As mixing continues, ethnic groups will continue to be shaped and formed. This is not the same as disappearing.

Looking at the situation from another point of view, American social problems may increase if mixing *doesn't* happen. Racial tensions are as high as they've ever been. Interracial families, however, ameliorate tensions by bringing diverse peoples together. If I had to choose between (1) greater separation of ethnic groups and increased hostility and (2) interracial mixing, transformed ethnic groups and decreased hostility, I'd take the latter.

Psychological and emotional health. Another argument given is that it's better for our psychological and emotional health to identify ourselves mainly with one race. Though it may not be explicitly stated, this reason is basically founded on physical appearance (as is the construct of race). Whichever race you favor is the race with which you should identify. You will be more able to deal with how you get treated if you identify this way.

Of course this stance raises some questions. What if I don't clearly

---

[4]Some American Indian tribes disappeared, but that was because they were murdered or killed by disease, not primarily because they interracially mixed with others. In fact, mixing enabled some tribes to survive.

look like one race or another? I know a young man who is a perfect blend of Korean and African American—he looks too Korean to be only black and too black to be only Korean. No matter which group he chooses to be with, his difference is conspicuous.

What if I look like a completely different racial group than the ones to which I biologically belong? I know a woman who is Filipina and white, but others consistently identify her as a Latina.

Or what if I look white? Will it be psychologically and emotionally easier for me if I just tell everyone I'm white? What if I look completely like my Latino family but identify more with my Asian one? Will it be easier if I live only as a Latino regardless of how I feel?

Ultimately this argument doesn't do any good for those whose appearance isn't clear cut or who, for whatever reason, don't feel comfortable identifying with only one race, even if they appear to be a "pure" member of that race.

Another facet of this "choose one" argument is that we all have a need to belong. (Sociologists would say we all need an "in-group.") If we identify with two or more groups, some say, we will remain adrift in a netherworld of racial ambiguity. Identifying with one, on the other hand, gives us that in-group we need to be healthy and well adjusted.

I would argue that it is possible to have multiple in-groups, and in fact most people do—just not multiple *racial* in-groups. We might find an in-group that is as racially diverse as we are. Or we might fill our need for belonging by joining an in-group that has nothing to do with race.

In the end there are no empirical data to support the argument that choosing one race will make us psychologically and emotionally healthier.

Power and politics. Politics and power dynamics provide another impetus for us to choose a race. A group, especially if it represents a minority within the larger society, generally wants numbers on its side and will claim anyone identified as being even remotely related and loyal to the cause. The message multiracial people often receive is "If you're with us then you need to be completely with us. You can't also be with them."

We need to break down this false dichotomy. Who *are* "us" and "them"? Determining this primarily on the basis of race and culture is dangerous, failing to consider that people can learn and change, and don't necessarily fit into perceptions about their ethnic or racial group.

On the other hand, social pressure to assimilate into dominant cultural ways of operating is very intense. It can be easy, too easy, for those of us who were raised around a lot of whites, or who look more white, not to rock the boat with white people even when we know we should. When this happens we take advantage of our status or appearance and perhaps receive superficial acceptance among whites, but at the cost of our wholeness—*and* that of our white brothers and sisters who need to be liberated from the degradation of racism and their ignorance of racial issues. We have not remained true to our full ethnic identity nor to our brothers and sisters of color who don't have the luxury of fading into a white crowd.

Interracial families and multiracial people will do well to partner with other ethnic minorities when it comes to fighting prejudice and inequities. We should do this because it's right, and also because we have been and are affected adversely by racism ourselves. It is aggravating and hurtful, however, to be viewed *only* as politically useful or harmful.

In spite of the fact that most multiracial people see themselves as ethnic minorities, the NAACP (National Association for the Advancement of Colored People) opposed a multiracial category on the census. So did the National Council of La Raza, the National Asian Pacific American Legal Consortium and the National Congress of American Indians (Mills and Grosz, p. 5). Why? Because it was unclear how the change would affect political redistricting, the enforcement of antidiscrimination legislation or the money given to programs aimed at reversing the effects of historical racism.

Indeed, because of the context in which we live, our choices as multiracial people automatically carry political implications. We need to be thoughtful about what we're choosing and why.

The Choice: This Side or That One?

One day at work, a Chinese-white friend of mine was asked how she wanted to be classified when employees were counted for government funding purposes. Minority or nonminority: those were the choices. "It was hard because I couldn't choose the nebulous 'other,'" she said. She felt illegitimate as a minority because she is "three-quarters" white, but she chose the minority category because she is also Chinese. She knows that not everyone agrees. A church acquaintance once told her, "You can't count that!" referring to her Chinese heritage.

Who decides what counts and what doesn't? For now, our world keeps us as fragmented racial parts that it can label, calculate and "understand"—count or discount, recruit or reject—instead of accepting our experiences for what they are and accepting us as enigmatic, valuable and whole human beings. It's a world that in many ways is not ready for us. Yet we're here, and more of us are coming.

How are we to see ourselves? How are we to relate to others? What are we to choose? Can we *change* our world?

Sometimes I think back on that first time I was publicly forced to pick a race, that summer day in Pasadena. I wonder what would have happened if I had refused to choose and had formed my own group of one person. I wonder.

For Reflection and Action

☐ When have you been asked or told to choose a race or ethnicity? How did it make you feel?

☐ How do you see yourself? How would you describe yourself? Write this down, and make sure that no matter what others think based on their evaluation, you know what you think.

☐ What choices have you voluntarily made about your racial and ethnic identity up to this point? What factors have most influenced your decision?

Oreo.
No thank you.
I'm not hungry right now.
Somehow the offering of this snack is the prelude to the ultimate attack.

Death by words is absurd to those who let letters drip from their tongues to form those questions forcing me to defend myself with justification for my existence on this colorful earth.

My birth
is not enough proof to the man who writes directions instructing me
to humbly
check the square that best describes me to a tee. I realize I am no longer protected by the privilege of my mother as I check OTHER. I aim to please when I attempt to squeeze my entire ancestry between those parallel and perpendicular lines forcing me to choose.

And I lose my freedom of choice as my voice echoes in the ears of my fellows.
Pick and choose
   one or the other
      my father or my mother
      my sister or my brother.
Live as black or as white or roam about shamefully in the shadows of gray.[5]

—LORI A. DINKINS

---

[5]Used by permission. Lori A. Dinkins is a writer, poet and former director of a company that provided diversity training in workplace and educational settings. I met Lori at the 1998 Colorlines Conference in Chicago, which brought together academics, activists and everyday people interested in discussing race and the development of a multiracial cohort in the United States.

2

Not Always As We Appear

When I was less than one year old, my newly married parents moved to Athens, Georgia. This relocation was not voluntary but an obligation to the U.S. Navy. The South in 1969 was not a particularly hospitable place for interracial couples—especially a black man and a white woman. When my parents left the base, they went with a mixed group of friends and could never hold hands or give any indication they were together.

One day my mom took me to the doctor for a regular checkup. He glanced at me next to my milky-white mother and declared, "This baby is eating too many yellow vegetables. Look at the color of her skin!" His diagnosis: I had "carotitis"—too much carotene in my diet. My mom had better watch what she was feeding me, or my skin would remain permanently discolored.

My mom kept her mouth shut. She was afraid of how we'd get treated if the doctor knew the real reason for my skin "discoloration."

Constant Comments
Chances are that if you're multiracial you've often been "misdiagnosed,"

and your looks have gotten you looks—puzzled, surprised, knowing and the second-take variety. They've probably also gotten you not a few unsolicited comments, many you could have done without. Maybe you've heard how attractive you are—and once they find out you're biracial, "Mixed people are always so good-looking."

Maybe you've heard "I never would've guessed"—about one or another of your races—or even outright questioning ("Are you really?"), as if you wouldn't be sure. Some come right out and ask, "What are you mixed with?" And then there's the indirect approach: "Where are you from?"—dancing around the topic of actual interest and trying hard not to seem nosy or rude.

Usually I get a triumphant "I *knew* it!" from satisfied inquisitors, as if they had unlocked one of the great mysteries of the universe.

Don't get me wrong, I really like talking about my biracial background with anyone who's interested in listening. However, some pretty crazy things have been said to me about how I look—things that would make *me* crazy if I let them.

New Acquaintance: "You're the most white-looking black person I've ever met."

Me (in my head): *Is that supposed to be a compliment? You obviously think I'm a freak of nature.*

New Acquaintance (white): "I never would have known you were black if you hadn't told me."

Me (in my head): *So are you going to treat me differently now?*

New Acquaintance (black): "You're really down with black culture, for a white woman."

Me (in my head): *Uggghhh, once again not recognized by my own people . . . what do I need to do, wear a sign?*

New Acquaintance (white): "So there must be some white on your black family's side, right?"

Me (in my head): *Why should I have to answer that question? I'm not interrogating you about your racial ancestry!*

Me (out loud): Yes, actually. My great-great-great grandfather was a master. He raped my great-great-great grandmother, one of his slaves.

Silence.

Me (in my head): *I thought that would do it.*

Fielding these comments and inquiries gets old after a while. But I've come to realize that I shake things up and that's just the way it is. I make people uncomfortable because who they thought I was is not who I am at all. When I think about it this way, I kind of like it that people are thrown off by my ambiguous appearance. I like challenging the status quo.

Being multiracial makes life interesting, but the truth is that multiracial people face a grave challenge. Because race traditionally has been founded on physical appearance, others assess where we belong in current racial categories based on our looks, regardless of how we see ourselves. They insist on using the current paradigm because that's what's known, what's comfortable. It's also the foundation of their identities; a change would be too destabilizing. Our challenge is to overcome such labeling by others, particularly based on how we look, and remain true to who we know we are.

Not Always Recognizable

"Identity: the condition or fact of being a certain person or thing *and recognizable as such*" (*Webster's II New Riverside Dictionary*, p. 346; emphasis added). As a biracial person, I find this dictionary definition interesting because my being African American is a certifiable fact even though many people do not recognize me as such. The definition reveals how deeply entrenched is the idea that one's appearance and identity ought to match—an assumption that is the source of much tension and pain for many multiracial people. Appearance is a huge factor in our experience of life because we are socially, though no longer legally, barred from claiming an identity that others cannot validate with their own eyes.

I have found it close to impossible to resist the assault of others' evaluations of my identity based on what *they* perceive. Yet that's what I have to do—daily. Judgments based on appearances are not a recent phenomenon, nor are they limited to the multiracial experience. Such judgments lie at the root of all prejudice and racism, and so in the end they are not a new problem but a very, very old one.

Michael Ramirez knows the pain of not being recognizable. "If somebody saw me they'd say I was 100 percent Mexican." But Michael's mother is Chinese, and so Michael is Chinese too, regardless of whether anyone else recognizes him as such. "I felt unknown," he said about his adolescent years. "I wanted people to know I was Chinese. I made a choice early in high school—I had to prove myself Chinese. I took any opportunity I had to let people know I knew the culture or slip in that my mom was Chinese."

Throughout high school Michael chose to join Asian American social circles and found acceptance. Among his friends he was seen as unique but "enough Asian to fit in."

His sophomore year he belonged to a tight group—eight Asian Americans (including himself) and one white. Michael remembers hearing one of the Asian Americans communicate a clear sense of superiority over their white friend. In response, Michael wanted even more to be seen as Asian. His pattern of having mostly Asian American friends continued through college.

Eventually Michael realized that his trying to prove himself "Asian enough" was at least partially a result of internalizing his friends' attitude of superiority. Michael revealed this realization to a former college roommate, another Chinese American. His friend confessed that sometimes he forgot Michael was Chinese. "You don't look it at all," he said.

The words hit Michael like a kick in the gut. It was supposed to be strangers who mistook him for a non-Asian—not his closest friends! Suddenly the awkwardness he had sometimes experienced with the former roommate made sense. He hadn't acknowledged it could have something to do with race, because he was working so hard to see himself as Chinese American too.

"You have fed into why I feel I have to prove myself," Michael told his old roommate. The feeling of being unknown hounded him again. Would his physical appearance always be the final issue for others?

It can be confusing when our looks don't line up with how we think of ourselves or are striving to think of ourselves. It is painful when we are branded as not belonging because we look different from the way people think we should. It especially hurts not to be recognized by those with whom we share racial heritage.

Once I attended a meeting for a newly forming think tank of black intellectuals, the Abyssinian Society. Unfortunately I arrived late, and no more seats were available around the large table where others had gathered. I took a chair along the wall of the meeting room and tried hard not to let the metaphor of being outside the circle take on too much meaning.

After a volley of remarks, a man commented how good it was to see three sisters in the room. Of course there were four if you counted me, but he didn't. Others who knew me intervened, making my presence known. The man looked embarrassed and mumbled, "Oh, I didn't see her," though our eyes had met when I walked into the room.

I didn't see her. It's tough being invisible to your own people, whether you're too light, too brown, too tall, too ambiguous, too whatever. After the meeting, I found an African American friend who I knew would understand and asked her to pray for me. Taking my painful experiences to friends and to God is how I have found solace and regained perspective when others' perceptions have thrown me off.

As much as it hurts to be judged by our looks, I've done the same to others. A couple of years ago I participated in a racism awareness seminar led by civil rights activist C. T. Vivian. Friends who had previously attended the seminar prepped me: Dr. Vivian didn't fool around—particularly with white people. The first morning he and his assistant, Kelly, came into the room dressed completely in black and looking *bad*. I was on edge, mostly because I anticipated not being recognized as one of the black people in the room.

During breaks, other black women would walk up to Kelly and chat and laugh freely. I found myself paralyzed by fear. *She's a militant black woman,* I thought. *Why would she want to talk to me? She probably thinks I'm a watered-down tragedy, not fit to belong to her race.*

At the end of the seminar, we each told the group how the experience had been for us. I cried as I described how difficult it was for me to sit through the sessions as a biracial person. The source of my pain was (and is) so deep it was difficult to articulate why I was crying, and my lack of self-control embarrassed me. Hearing the confessions of whites and the anger of blacks had stirred up a lot. Feeling invisible in the conversation had stirred up even more.

Afterward Kelly came to me and told me that she had really felt for me throughout the two days (I guess she could tell I was in pain). She hadn't said anything earlier because she knew I needed to go through what I was going through. Even more surprising than her initiative and compassion was what she laid on me next: she was biracial too!

I was mortified and ashamed at how quickly *I* had succumbed to appearances, making all sorts of assumptions based solely on looks— exactly what I don't want others to do to me.

None of us is immune from making judgments based on appearances. Of anyone, multiracial people should be aware that looks say little about a person's true identity. Yet how often we forget this, especially about ourselves.

How Our Looks Affect Our Identity

How you look has undoubtedly gotten you some attention—some positive, some negative. Regardless of what kind of attention you've received, your self-identity has been affected. It's a fact of how we've been created—our identity is affected by how others reflect ourselves back to us, what they do and don't remark on, and the content of those remarks.

"Most people don't see me as just Anglo," said one Chinese-white woman. "I've gotten Jewish, Greek, Italian, Hispanic. I had a high school counselor who spoke Spanish to me every time I went in. She kept forgetting I wasn't Hispanic." When she visited a black church, an acquaintance there asked her, "So you're black and what else?"

The only people who immediately recognize her as part Asian are other part Asians, she said. Others' failure to see the Chinese in her has made it difficult for her to assert being Chinese. "It's made it harder for me to feel confident because I don't have the looks to back up the claim." On the other hand, she has always had a strong biracial identity. Others' reactions to her appearance have underscored for her that she's not exclusively white.

A Jewish-black woman with brown skin told me, "When I was

younger I wished I looked more biracial because I wanted to be hard to categorize." She wanted people to have to ask questions. "I thought it was cool to be biracial, and I didn't want people to take that away." She also didn't feel that she totally fit into the black community, and looking different might give her more latitude not to fit.

In retrospect, she knows that her desires were not about looks but about having the freedom to be herself. "It was a means to an end, in my mind. I didn't really want to change how I looked." When asked how she identifies herself now she says, "I am African American and biracial—fully both.

"I used to think of myself as black and white, since I had one parent of each. I had a very literal understanding." This has changed as she has faced reality in America as a brown-skinned woman. "I need to make some allowance for how race and ethnicity function in our society, even if I won't let it fully define me."

To others Pete Almeida Jr. looks like a black man, which he is. Pete sees himself as black too, yet he wonders if there's more to him than that one label describes. "Socially and culturally I've been raised black. I look in the mirror and see black," he says. Pete was adopted at six months and raised by black parents of Cape Verdean[1] and West African descent.

As a teen, Pete discovered that not only was he adopted, he was biracial. His biological mother was Jewish, and his father was Cape Verdean. The news introduced another level of turmoil to his life, but it didn't change his racial identity. He had always been black to himself and others, and he remained so.

Pete went to the University of Rhode Island and joined a Christian group that was predominantly white. "I knew no other Christians on campus and I desired fellowship with like-minded people. I didn't care much about their color. I didn't know many black students or other stu-

---

[1]Cape Verde is an archipelago off the western coast of Africa. The Portuguese settled the islands in 1462. The country remained a Portuguese colony for five hundred years and was considered important to the trans-Atlantic slave trade. The population is presently two-thirds Creole (mixed-race European and African). Many Cape Verdeans have migrated and established communities in Rhode Island.

dents of color who were strong Christians." He stayed involved with the group throughout college and after graduating was asked to come on staff with the ministry.

Around this time Pete served as a counselor at a summer orientation program for students of color entering URI. During a cultural talent show, Cape Verdeans and African Americans did separate presentations. Pete was assigned to the former, because the people in charge knew he was of Cape Verdean descent. His unfamiliarity with Cape Verdean culture and history, however, superseded his heritage. "I felt like a foreigner," Pete says. "I couldn't speak the language, I didn't know the dances or the music." The experience threw him off. "I felt insecure, flushed, my heart was palpitating. I thought, *I'm black, I should be with the African American students.*"

On staff with the campus ministry, he agreed to focus primarily on ministering to black students because there was a need for that. He quickly discovered that this threw him off too. He had always seen himself as black, but put in a position of having to lead, he wasn't sure others would follow. "I didn't know how to minister to people of color because I didn't feel black enough." Pete's multiracial background started haunting him. "I felt like an alcoholic—'Hi, I'm Pete and I'm biracial.' . . . That's only part of who I am, but I felt like I had to say it."

Over time, relationships with mature and accepting black Christians increased his confidence about his identity. "My exposure to black Christians affirmed who I was, a Christian of African descent." He also went to Atlanta for a summer to work with an urban ministry program. "Black people were running things—mature, godly people. That affirmed some stuff in me."

Pete knows his identity is still in process, though. "All through college I considered myself an African American. Now I say I'm biracial." He has mixed feelings about exploring his Cape Verdean heritage ("Maybe I'll feel less black"). On the other hand, he thinks that meeting his Jewish mother might bring him some much-needed resolution. His reaction to the movie *Schindler's List* caught him off guard. "I cried at the end. It was weird, thinking that they might be my relatives. It felt like a part of me is missing, and I want to know if I had people over there in the concentration camps."

Pete is more than he appears. Like all of us, he is trying to reconcile who he and others have expected him to be with who he actually is.

Accepting Our Appearance and Our Selves

Our appearance has played a role in our ethnic identity development. It has affected our self-perceptions, others' perceptions of us and how much dissonance we have experienced over who we are. The exact relationship between our looks and our identity choices, however, is unpredictable because we are all so different. There will not always be, nor does there need to be, a correlation between how we look and our ultimate ethnic identity.

In one study of binational Amerasians (people with an Asian parent from Asia and a white or black American parent), researchers found that darker-skinned Afroasians did not automatically relate to African Americans. Neither did lighter-skinned Afroasians necessarily identify themselves readily as Japanese.

One woman with an Asian parent and a white parent who looked Anglo, but who spoke and understood only limited English, identified herself as being more Japanese than anything else. She *looked* Anglo, but her social and psychological makeup was far more Japanese in orientation (Root, *Racially Mixed People*, p. 291).

Feeling (and being) different is an inevitable part of multiracial and multiethnic existence. Even if no one ever pointed it out, most of us would realize that our experience is divergent from that of the majority of people around us whose parents are of the same race. Usually, however, others do point out our difference quite frequently. This makes some depressed, others obsessively self-conscious. The goal is to think of ourselves rightly—no better than others because of our racial makeup, and definitely no worse. Being different can actually help our self-esteem once we accept that differences can be good.

George Kitahara Kich, a clinical psychologist and cofounder of I-Pride, an interracial family organization, has actively introduced the issue of biracial identity among Asian Americans and others. He identifies three stages in the development of a biracial, bicultural identity, starting with a consciousness of being different:

1. an initial awareness of differentness and dissonance between self-perceptions and others' perceptions of them (initially, three through ten years of age)

2. a struggle for acceptance from others (initially, eight through late adolescence and young adulthood)

3. acceptance of themselves as people with a biracial and bicultural identity (late adolescence throughout adulthood)

Kich notes that these stages repeat cyclically, often with greater intensity and awareness. He concludes, "The major developmental task for biracial people is to differentiate critically among others' interpretations of them, various pejorative and grandiose labels and mislabels, and their own experiences and conceptions of themselves" (Root, *Racially Mixed People*, pp. 305-6).

Three stages and a concluding statement are much easier to identify than to live by, but they point to a path for us to walk. We need to distinguish between what others think of us and what we know of ourselves (sometimes others will have it right, but often they won't). Then we must accept the truth of who we are and not try to be someone else. When we start to do these things, we are on our way to loving ourselves as people whom God has made multiracial and multicultural.

Note that the last stage—acceptance—goes on *throughout* adulthood. It is OK to be struggling with this. You are not abnormal, nor are you alone in your struggle.

Pete Almeida Jr. is working out what it means to be himself, five years after graduating from college. "Being biracial—Jewish and Cape Verdean—I am probably more of European than of African descent. But when I look in the mirror and how I am perceived by society I will always be a black man. I want to affirm all of who I am. I am a work in process. Although the Scripture says we are fearfully and wonderfully made and made perfectly in God's image, I am still coming to terms with that. But I do think God has allowed me to connect with folks from different cultures from literally all over the world. I would not trade those experiences in for anything. Those folks have enriched my life.

"I am learning not to apologize for who I am but trust God has used and will continue to use my background and life experiences for his purposes. Come to think of it, maybe many biracials are just modern-day Moses stories waiting to happen." Pete points out that Moses was not biracial by birth but definitely by upbringing and then adds, "And we all know how the story ended with him."

For me, accepting my appearance has been one of the most difficult aspects of being biracial. It starts with feeling self-conscious that I stand out too much in a black context and not enough in a white one. And then the thoughts begin, *If only my hair were a little more "black." If only my skin were darker.* After that comes frustration or even anger that my appearance betrays me. Then guilt for wishing for something other than what God has given me, and fear that my mom would be hurt if she knew how I sometimes feel.

The three things that have helped me the most in this battle to accept my appearance and ultimately myself are (1) recognition from other blacks, (2) reaching out to and caring for others, and (3) friends of all races who see my heart—who I really am—and like and accept me for *me.*

Being recognized versus being recognizable. At a national conference for black students I helped to staff, I had three roommates with whom I really hit it off. We stayed up until two, three, even four in the morning having deep conversations about race, skin color, interracial relationships, relationships between black women and, of course, hair. One night during one of these conversations, it dawned on me that I didn't feel like an "outsider" listening to three "insiders"—I was an insider too. There were many levels on which I could have identified with these women: as a woman, as an employee of the same organization, as a Christian. But I knew I was mostly connecting racially, as a *black* woman, and it felt good.

I told them this, and they were excited with me. The next day one of them said, "I want you to know that when I look at you I see a beautiful black woman." She is a good friend who values my biracial identity and ultimately likes me as "Sundee," but at that particular moment she wanted to affirm the bond we share as sisters of African descent.

At another event I experienced recognition and affirmation from black people as I led worship. A woman came up to me one night and told me she saw and enjoyed the leadership gifts God had given me. She ended her encouragement with "And this little black face just came by to remind you of this."

At that moment I burst out crying, leaving the woman, Skip, perplexed. Through my blubbering I told her I was crying because I have a huge fear that my light skin gets in the way of other blacks' receiving the gifts I have to offer. It meant a lot, therefore, for her to tell me she enjoyed my leadership. Since then Skip has become a very close friend and mentor.

Another way to gain recognition from a community is to identify with them explicitly. I once told a group of black coworkers that I see myself as an "undercover black person." I would not always be recognized as black, but I was with them when it came to fighting racism. And as often as I can, I take advantage of my involuntary social position as a light-skinned person in America to question or challenge the misconceptions and prejudices that I'm privy to because people don't think of me in the way they think of other blacks.

A tough reality I have had to face, however, is that because of how I look I have undoubtedly escaped much of the outright hostility, cold indifference and awkward discomfort that my darker black brothers and sisters face daily. I don't know how it feels to have my competence doubted because of my skin color. I don't understand how it feels to have the dynamics in a room full of whites change when I walk in. (Though I have often wondered what both whites and blacks are thinking when my interracial family walks into a room.)

My black pastor once told me never to wish mistreatment based on race upon myself. I know he's right. But I have wanted to be able to say I know how it feels. I have wanted to experience the psychic bond that skin-color discrimination forges between people. Instead I have experienced discrimination indirectly, realizing that whenever a black person is unfairly treated, mistrusted or underestimated on the basis of race, it is in essence an offense against me—because I am black, too, *whether or not others recognize me as such*.

A Mexican-Irish friend says most people assume he's white. Like me, he is learning to use this to address racial issues with other whites. "Sometimes when white people find out I'm half Mexican, I somehow become this spokesman for all Latinos or sometimes for all minorities. I don't like that, but sometimes I realize that I may be the only minority they'd ever really listen to, so I try to take that responsibility seriously." He usually points out that he can't speak for all Latinos, but he'll give his opinion on what prevailing feelings are in the Latino community if he's aware of them. To the extent he's able, he tries to explain why some Latinos feel as they do. "Oftentimes I'm the only Mexican they really know, and that's only because they didn't spot me as one in the first place!"

In his first couple years of college, my friend became more aware of racial issues and how they affected people, especially in urban American settings. "At times I keyed in on the ways that the white race in America has benefited at the expense of minorities, and my initial reaction was to wish that I was pure Mexican. I wanted to be on the moral high ground, not to be connected to or a beneficiary of, and therefore not responsible for, the oppression of the past and the legacy of oppressive situations in the present."

Over time, however, he gained a new understanding of the access he had to certain resources because he was white. "Being half Mexican . . . gave me a perspective on the oppressive ways that those resources have been used, and a motivation to use them in the service of justice instead, as well as insight on what kinds of help would be most beneficial to minorities and Mexicans in particular. So now I'm glad that I'm biracial."

Reaching out to others. As I get to know God better, I am coming to understand why Jesus put the command to love others on the same level as the command to love God. God has it set up so that we become more whole the more we help others to become whole. If we don't actively seek to care for others, we remain half people, miserably focused only on ourselves. Jesus knows this, and since he wants us to be whole and to have joy and life, he tells us to love others. All of my identity woes are put in perspective each time I enter into the suffering of others or reach out to another struggling human being.

The summer internships I have spent teaching kids in the city, showing them I care about them and taking time to play with them, have been the most healing times of my life. The children experienced my love, and I experienced their acceptance—healing all around. My racial background may have come up once or twice, but in the end I was foremost an adult who cared. When I volunteered for a ministry helping women of all races to get out of prostitution and off drugs, it didn't matter what race I was. It mattered that I was there.

As I have taken time to get to know and care for other black women, particularly, the depth of self-hatred I've seen in what they sometimes say about themselves has astounded me. "I wish I had hair like yours," I've heard more than once. Every time I see this self-hatred or hear comparative comments like the one about my hair, I am convicted again of how important it is that I accept and like myself so that I have the emotional resources to reassure others who are struggling to like how they look.

Offering the gift of myself to others has reinforced that I am not a racial category but a human being, made in the likeness of God, created to love and be loved. Furthermore, I am a *gift*. And I am not as prone to fret about whether my wrapping looks right or has enough of this or that color when I am experiencing the fulfillment of caring for others.

Friends who see your heart. True friends have been the most powerful agents of wholeness in my life: people who like my racial makeup but who, when they hug me, embrace my heart and not just my physical self. These friends see deeper than my achievements or my insecurities and deficiencies.

One night when I was struggling with self-acceptance, two good friends made me say five things I liked about myself. I broke down crying. It just seemed too hard of a task; I was sure anything I came up with wouldn't be true or worthwhile. But my friends wouldn't budge—they saw what I couldn't see.

I sniffled and stammered and resisted some more, but I knew what I wanted to say first. "I like that I'm biracial."

They smiled and nodded. I could tell that they liked this about me too. It felt good to acknowledge that I enjoy this part of me, and to have it affirmed by others.

After a few more torturous moments, I got out all five things, and then one of them said, "Now, I want you to thank God regularly for the good ways he's made you."

That was a radical concept! I'd heard of thanking God before. But thanking God for me? The idea seemed a little "out there," but I was intrigued. Ultimately I knew my friends were right. My thoughts toward myself needed to be completely reprogrammed, and proactive gratefulness for myself was necessary. I thank God for who I am and for all of my wise and caring friends who have seen into my heart and loved me for me.

If you're like me, you've spent some time in front of the mirror scrutinizing every square inch to discern which parts of you are from what race. It's not easy to stop worrying about how we look. Maybe you've pored over extended-family photographs seeking your nose, your eyes, your lips. Do I have my white grandfather's nose or my black grandmother's? I might be light-skinned, but look at me next to my black dad—we've got the exact same face shape and body build!

In the end, this kind of searching will most likely lead to frustration and deception rather than revelation, or the ultimate goal—self-acceptance. Physical characteristics are not the keys to discovering our racial and ethnic selves. No one race has exclusive rights to almond-shaped eyes, a wide nose or high cheekbones.

I've come to accept that I've got a little of my mom and my dad in my smile, a little of my mom and my dad in my eyes. My mom and my dad, and multitudes of ancestors for that matter, are running all throughout my body, evident in the small subtleties of who I am, not just my skin color or hair texture or other parts that people notice. I've got my mom's fingers and my dad's toes (a fact that has my husband fearing my feet thirty years from now). Whether my features are "black" or "white" doesn't affect the truth that I am, and always will be, a mixture of black and white.

I've learned that regardless of who I look like or what race my face favors, it's crucial that I accept myself completely. I can lie in the sun all day, but my facial features aren't going to change. (Speaking of which, I encourage you never to alter your appearance with surgery—you won't be any happier until you deal with the internal issues of how you feel about yourself.) I can get a tighter curl with a perm, which I've tried, but it won't change the texture of my hair. I need to like myself because my Creator likes me. If others have a problem with my looks I'll just go on being myself, and either I'll win them over, or they'll miss out on knowing a great person.

There has never been nor will there ever be another you in the history of the world. Now that's amazing.

"The biracial person's ability to create congruent self-definitions rather than be determined by others' definitions and stereotypes may be said to be the major achievement of a biracial and bicultural identity" (Root, *Racially Mixed People,* p. 314). Like any major achievement, this one will take time—a lifetime even. Try to enjoy the process and let it make you stronger.

As you grow into self-acceptance, there is One who understands to whom you can always turn. Jesus, though he was indeed the Son of God, was not recognized as such. Though he was the King of kings, he "had no form or majesty that we should look at him, nothing in his appearance that we should desire him" (Is 53:2). He knows how it feels not to be accepted or considered legitimate based on appearance. This lack of recognition, however, didn't keep him from knowing and being who he was.

God, not others, determines reality, including who we are ethnically. He has made us a mixture whether others accept that or not. We can turn to him for comfort and guidance in knowing and being who we are—with recognition or without.

For Reflection and Action

As you go through the process of determining who you are apart from others' perceptions of you, perhaps these suggestions will help.

☐ Consider how you feel about your appearance. Reject the lies that have been implanted by others' remarks ("I'm too light to be _____," or "I look too black to be Asian"). Then think about the positives associated with your experience ("My skin color gives me greater access to situations where I can challenge racism," or "I can help broaden people's definitions of what it means to be black *and* what it means to be Asian.")

☐ Write a poem or some kind of reminder of your true and growing identity that you can keep posted in a visible place. I've got a sign in the office where I write that says, "I'm black and I'm proud! I'm white and I'm proud! I'm biracial and I'm proud!"

☐ Craft comebacks to comments that you've grown to expect. One that has worked when people comment on how light I am: "I guess I challenge the notion that we can tell who people are by how they look." Or if I'm talking to a black person: "You know we come in all colors!" These comebacks prevent me from internalizing messages that aren't helpful to my self-image, which includes that I am black as well as white.

☐ Memorize this word of wisdom from the Bible: "The LORD does not see as mortals see; they look on the outward appearance, but the LORD looks on the heart" (1 Sam 16:7). Work on your character, which you *can* change, and stop worrying about physical attributes which you can't.

☐ If you have experienced lack of recognition or acceptance from one of your ethnic groups, ask God for an ally from that group. God will send friends your way who accept you as biracial and also affirm the part of you that they share with you.

☐ Reach out to others and see how much you have to offer them, regardless of how you—or they—look.

☐ Seek friends who love your heart, who you *really* are.

who am i?

who am i?
am i who i say i am?
or am i something else?
He who calls Himself the great "I am,"
YAHWEH,
or I-am-Who-I-am,
tells me that i'm free to be who i am.
and yet i question myself.
am i?

if i were who i am—
would it be okay,
alright,
or right?
can i really be part mexican and part white?

but i'm way too lite,
sight to be seen,
some would say the brown's been washed clean.
but i know who i am.
and i know that a part of my heart's fully a brown part.
and i love my mom's family,
that beautiful we that's such a part of the "i am" that's me.

and so i'm torn.
born to be who i am
but sometimes forlorn.
i'll try to be who i am
helped only by Him
who's the great "I am."[2]

—NATHAN BAIRD

---

[2]Nathan Baird grew up in Atwater, an Air Force base town in California's Central Valley. His maternal grandmother is Mexican and his other grandparents are of mixed European descent. Nathan wrote and recited this poem in February 2001 at the first-ever conference for multiracial students from colleges and universities in the Los Angeles area, a conference at which I spoke.

3

How Can I Be Many in One?

Johnathan Perkins was just following instructions. He didn't mean to make things difficult the day his sixth-grade teacher counted her students by race.

From the front of the room she told all the black boys to stand up. *That's me,* Johnathan thought, standing. The teacher scratched a number on her paper. Johnathan wondered why it mattered what race they were.

"White boys, please stand," she said.

That's me too, Johnathan said to himself as he thought about his white mom and all his Mennonite relatives in Pennsylvania. He stood, a little self-conscious about what the other black kids might think.

His teacher looked at him, nonplussed. Necks craned, and eyes registered confusion. But Johnathan stood his ground. "I wasn't trying to prove a point. . . . If I only stood up for one it would mean that I was saying I wasn't the other," he said later, matter-of-factly. "It was embarrassing—the fact that everyone was looking at me—but I felt proud that I wasn't lying about who I was."

After class, the teacher asked Johnathan why he had stood for both. "Because I *am* both," he said.

She said she didn't know and she was sorry to have put him in that predicament. But she could only count him once so that the numbers would add up.

Johnathan is very aware of having a "both/and" identity and he stands by it, even if it confuses others or messes up their numbers.

Maintaining a multiracial identity in our racially polarized world isn't easy. As my Korean-white friend Erna once said, "Sometimes I want to get off this biracial train!" Though on one level multiracial people symbolize racial unity and God's work to bring races together, even "in one body" (Eph 2:16), we experience the existing "walls of hostility" (Eph 2:14) starkly and personally. As Erna put it, "The cliché that we *are* racial reconciliation is not really true. I feel 'the dividing wall of hostility' *within* me."

Developing an identity is tough for anyone. However, the identity development task is tougher in one way for multiracial people: some of the ethnic groups to which we owe our lives are historic enemies and remain in conflict with one another. To be both American Indian and white, both Korean and Japanese, both Jewish and Gentile, or a hundred other combinations, when these groups remain hostile toward (or even just aloof from) one another, is a strain. Even Asians and whites, or Latinos and blacks, who would appear to have greater affinity with each other in the United States, hold stereotypes, fears and animosities toward one another that make being both Asian and white, or both Latino and black, difficult.

Our world remains racially divided, and this *external* problem makes it difficult for us to develop a positive identity. Maria P. P. Root, a leading researcher in the field of multiracial families and individuals, puts it this way: "It is the marginal status imposed by society rather than the objective mixed race of biracial individuals which poses a severe stress to positive identity development" (Root, *Racially Mixed People*, p. 78). In other words, *you are not the problem.* There is nothing inherently wrong with being racially or ethnically mixed.

To find wholeness, we need to reconcile and integrate our different heritages, histories and present racial and ethnic realities, even when our choices and actions confuse others. The goal is to find the identities that fit and that are true to reality, to know who we are and to accept ourselves as we are so that we can live out our God-given purposes.

If you don't take time to know, develop and accept who you are, you will not live very happily and you will not be available to fulfill your purpose in this world and in others' lives. You'll be too busy obsessing about whether you're all right and securing acceptance from others.

Along the way to an identity that fits, it is normal to want and need help. We are striving to maintain multiple racial, ethnic and cultural identities within our one person—identities that in the external world are in conflict. One place we can turn is to other multiracial people.

This chapter includes stories of three people from whom we can gain insights about the process of developing a multiracial and multi-ethnic identity. The Israelite leader Moses will also serve as an example of someone who had to work out his ethnicity, and finally I will offer some personal reflections about what it's meant to be "many in one." We will discover that there are multiple ways to be a multiracial person.

Catching Culture

The daughter of a Chinese-white mother and white father, Alexis Spencer-Byers is biracial.

In her San Francisco high school, Alexis's social group was a mix of Asian Americans and whites. Even though she knew and liked that she was biracial, she perceived herself as being more culturally white, not knowing the Chinese language and only some of the food.

Then as a teen, she saw *The Joy Luck Club* with her mom. It changed her self-view forever. "We cried through the whole thing. Afterwards, we couldn't talk about it. The film raised issues that were too painful to discuss. Some things [in the movie] any mom and daughter could have related to—but it felt like more, it felt ethnic." The movie became a touchstone for Alexis. In it she found points of identification that told her she was culturally *Asian* too.

In college she grew close to two biracial peers, one Korean-white and the other Japanese-white. It encouraged all three of them that they recognized each other immediately as *hapa* (a multiracial person with Asian heritage). They had an affinity that Alexis hadn't experienced with monoracial friends.

Her Korean-white friend participated in the Asian American group on campus but never felt fully accepted. As a result, Alexis avoided the group. "I thought, *If half isn't considered good enough, there's no way a quarter is going to cut it.*"

Her Asian heritage, however, was still very important to her. Over time, as she learned about Chinese cultural values, it stunned her to realize how much they had influenced her without her knowing it. She hadn't been taught Chinese culture, but through her mom and grandma she had caught it.

Now she could articulate what she had in common with the Asian women in *The Joy Luck Club.* "In the movie, there's a woman who can't allow herself to want anything. She's desperately trying to figure out what her husband wants and what he wants her to want." Alexis identified heart and soul with this character. While she knows that self-definition is a struggle for most women, she has become aware that Asian women struggle with it even more because of what the culture teaches. Realizing this commonality helped her to feel that "there's a sense of solidarity, like at least I'm not the only one. Some of the others who are dealing with this are also Asian women, and we need to overcome together."

Alexis discovered that she is motivated by shame and that she's tremendously willing to sacrifice for the sake of her family—both Chinese cultural traits. When her mom needed help caring for Alexis's younger sister, who has Down syndrome, Alexis left college for a year. Her white friends responded with shock: "You're doing *what?* Are you sure you don't want to think about it some more? You're not going to graduate with your class!" Her decision came at a cost, but she didn't labor long over it. Now she understands that her ability to value family over individual pursuits is a gift of one of her ethnicities.

Alexis has also realized that she can be quite self-effacing. This Asian way of presenting herself doesn't always work in mainstream American settings. At one company where she worked, employees received annual bonuses based on their performance evaluations. "Of course I rated myself considerably lower than I thought I actually deserved, figuring it was better to start low and let [my supervisor] go up than the other way around. I wouldn't want to appear conceited, after all. [My supervisor], I suppose trusting that I as an American would give myself at least my due, turned it in exactly as I had completed it. Good thing I'm not in this for the money!"

After graduating from Amherst College, Alexis moved to Jackson, Mississippi. "Throughout high school and college I was in situations where there were almost as many Asians as whites. I took it for granted. When I came to Jackson I had to represent Asians to blacks and whites. The [Asian] culture was around me in San Francisco and Amherst. In Mississippi, if it's not *within* me it's missing. I've had to make it my own."

Alexis caught more culture than she originally knew. Now she is taking steps to regain elements lost to her when her grandmother immigrated to the United States. She is learning the language, planning a trip to China with her mom and trying to meet other Chinese Americans.

Some of us have caught more culture than we currently know. Learning about our ethnic cultures will help us see what of them is already in us and solidify our sense of having a multiethnic identity.

Embracing Our Ethnicity

Michael Ramirez grew up in Hacienda Heights, a suburb of East Los Angeles. Both his Chinese mother and his Mexican father spoke Spanish at home, so Michael spoke Spanish almost exclusively. His aunts babysat him and his brother regularly, giving him increased exposure to Mexican culture.

When Michael went to kindergarten, however, he discovered that all his classmates spoke only English. He no longer wanted to speak Spanish. This experience set the stage for what Michael would experience throughout school—a lack of desire to be associated with his Mexican side.

Though Michael describes himself as looking Mexican, and his high school as equally Asian, Latino and white, by adolescence 90 percent of his friends were Asian. This was partly because he was tracked in classes where a majority of the students were Asian.

Michael also had his own biases. "I saw Latino kids in gangs, and I didn't want to be associated with them. They were the troublemakers, and I didn't want to be seen as that." He and a biracial Latino-white friend would joke that they had gotten the white and Asian brain instead of the Mexican one. Michael wanted to avoid the stigma attached to being Mexican, and he longed for his classmates to accept him as Asian American.

His Chinese grandparents moved close by, and even though he couldn't communicate with them because of the language barrier, he saw many characteristics in them that he liked. They were generous and devoted to family. His grandma would serve huge, delicious meals. His Mexican grandparents had died before he got to know them. Michael continued to see himself primarily as Chinese and to ignore his Mexican side.

After his junior year in college, Michael took a trip to work with a student group at a Latino church in Detroit. They spent part of their summer visiting shut-ins, and Michael had many long conversations with two elderly Latina women. Their experiences touched something in him. The child who spoke Spanish as his first language and was cared for by Mexican aunts was being reawakened.

At the end of the summer, the pastor brought Michael's group forward during a church service. Michael looked out at the Latino congregation. For the first time he saw a group of Latinos as *his* people. This was only the beginning of a huge shift in Michael's ethnic identity. He would need to confront his own racism in a much deeper way.

After graduating from college, he attended a conference centered on racial healing and reconciliation. In one session participants were given the opportunity to confess their racism. This was nothing new for Michael, since his Christian group on campus had openly discussed race and racism. He didn't expect any new insight to surface in him.

Suddenly a thought popped into Michael's mind. *He was racist toward Latinos.* Michael had never considered this before. He had convinced himself that he simply identified more with his Chinese side.

A deep sense of shame came over him. He feared the reality that he could be racist even against himself. "The whole idea of [biracial] people being reconciliation—I'm not that. Racism had shaped my identity,"

Michael said. But there was no ignoring what God was saying: Michael needed to deal with his internalized racism and his feelings about being Latino.

After this, the conference broke into ethnic-specific groups. The first time this had happened, Michael had gone with the Asian Americans. Now Michael knew he needed to go with the Latinos. He joined the small group and found himself warmly welcomed and fairly comfortable. It was a small but significant step of repentance and healing.

Since Michael's junior year of college he had facilitated discussions for Latino students at the request of his Christian group's leader. He sometimes didn't enjoy these times because he didn't relate, especially when the others talked passionately about being victims of racism. He had led the meetings mainly because there was a need.

After being convicted of his own racism, however, he returned to leading these discussions with an awareness of *his* need to change. He also began coordinating Latino "family nights" on campus, as a volunteer for the Christian group. "This is what I need and what will bring healing to my racism," he said. "I'm seeing again what I like about Latino culture."

Michael decided that he needed to learn more about the Mexican side of his family. His parents had never talked with him about his racial identity. He took his dad to lunch and asked him questions: Why had he come to the United States? What was he like when he was younger? What was his father (Michael's grandfather) like? Pride in his dad's Mexican heritage grew. Michael learned that his dad prized family. He'd sacrificed greatly to bring his sisters to the United States and had worked very hard to get where he was. Michael's dad hadn't been back to his hometown for twenty-five years. They talked about taking a road trip to visit relatives there.

"The more that I'm around Mexican people, the more I love being Mexican," Michael said. On a recent weekend trip to Mexico he realized that values he thought were Chinese, such as generosity, are Mexican also. He hopes to regain his Spanish fluency and is moving into a Latino neighborhood—something he knows he needs to do, given what God is doing in his life. "I still have a lot to figure out, but my desire is to see myself as totally Chinese *and* Mexican, and to understand what that means. I want to have a deep peace about it."

Michael also plans on teaching kindergarten, the grade at which he started to cut off his Mexican self. Perhaps he will be able to encourage the children in his class to embrace every part of their ethnicity.

Some of us have a hard time identifying with one of our ethnic groups because we're ashamed. Michael provides an example of how we can root out our internalized racism on our way to a multiethnic identity.

Racial Realities

"I was always different. I can't remember not being different," says Amanda Beckenstein of Philadelphia. "But I felt special. People would ask, 'Do you celebrate Hanukkah or Christmas?' and I'd say, 'Both,' and I was like 'Yeah!'"

Her parents didn't tell her she was both Jewish and black. In fact, her African American mom taught her to identify herself only as black. "She was always trying to give me racial identity. . . . She'd ask, 'Why don't you have more black friends?' or 'Why do you listen to this music?'"

Amanda realizes in retrospect that her mother was preparing her to survive in a society hostile to blacks. Amanda, however, didn't see where she was raised as particularly hostile. Columbia, Maryland, was a planned community developed in the 1960s to foster socioeconomic and ethnic diversity and peaceful coexistence. She had never felt the need to defend herself as a black person there. "Self-hatred and color-consciousness weren't a part of my thinking, so [my mom] was trying to counteract something that wasn't there. . . . It wouldn't occur to me *not* to have black pride."

At age seven Amanda started going to a black church. She told the Sunday school teacher she was half Jewish, and it would some-times come up. "We're all Gentiles—except Amanda," the teacher would say, making Amanda proud. Over time, though, Amanda experienced herself not fitting in with the other black children, a feeling she didn't like. She still doesn't know if the primary source of this tension was cultural—the result of being biracial—or if it was just, as she says, "the nerd thing."

Her social involvements in college reflected her refusal to be pigeon-holed. She participated in The Sisterhood, a black group; a Jewish singing group; and The Other Box, a multiracial/multicultural group. Yet she still longed to feel greater belonging in the black community. As a first-year student, she got the impression from another black woman that there were standards and expectations she needed to meet to be accepted by blacks on campus.

After college, while at a gathering of her organization's black employees, it finally sank in to Amanda that she had belonged all along. At this gathering, she said later, "we were of so many different backgrounds, worship styles and cultures—and that was OK. That was the first time I could be in a room full of black people and not feel performance anxiety." There were others who had felt similar pressures as her, who had grown up in white environments and could relate to elements of white culture. She realized she could still be black, even with her biracial heritage and multicultural upbringing.

The next year, in the midst of facing blatant racism from white Christians, Amanda realized, "I needed to stop the 'dance of accommodation.' I'd been systematically erasing experiences to make white people feel better." Suddenly she was encountering what her mother had assumed she would encounter much earlier, and she responded the way her mother expected—with anger and a deeper connection to her African American identity. "It caused me . . . to call upon the resources of history—the struggles others have had and how they dealt with them.

"When all that was happening, it was very hard to be biracial. . . . Being biracial makes everything personal. I can't be mad at my white family," she says. "[Being biracial] never lets me make blanket assumptions about people. I could, but it makes it psychologically inconvenient." Instead of being angry with individuals, she found herself getting angry at a seminary that in her mind epitomized individuals who are unaware of and unconcerned about racism in the United States. It was easier to be mad at an institution.

Racial realities and others' racism have shaped Amanda's identity. "Now I'm trying to figure out how I fit into the present in relation to history. I relate to 'Eastern European Jew' more than 'white.' . . . I'm not less than African American, but at the same time I still appreciate all my ethnic and cultural heritage. I haven't lost any interest in my Jewish heritage." In fact, she found her Hebrew seminary class so interesting that she's pursuing a Ph.D. in Hebrew Bible, a decision definitely influenced by her ancestral connection.

Some of us, simply because of how we look, cannot avoid the reality of racism. Like Amanda, we need to work out having multiethnic identities in the midst of people's perceptions and personal and societal racism.

As Alexis, Michael and Amanda discover, develop and accept who they are, they are finding and fulfilling their purposes. And so can you. Our stories are diverse and yet similar in that we all seek to be at peace with ourselves.

Toward a "Many in One" Identity

"I am what I am." Before you can be at peace with yourself and live out your purpose, *you* need to accept who you are. I am learning that what others think of me is not nearly as significant, nor will it have as long-lasting an impact on my life, as what I feel and think about myself. Usually, if we're honest, the reason we're not OK with ourselves is that we care too much about other people's opinions. We make race more important than accepting ourselves and believing that God made us and accepts us as we are.

You may have difficulty accepting a non-European part of yourself—a consequence of racism in our society. You may reject your European-descended self, in backlash against that same racism, or because European American culture is ubiquitous, hard to define and sometimes seems about as interesting as its moniker, "white bread."

Race is a messed-up paradigm in many ways, but it and its effects are too real to ignore. There is neither a wholesale evil race nor a superior race, so we can accept our racial selves in all of their beautiful mixed glory. Despite pervasive societal messages to the contrary, racial identity is not tantamount to total identity. You are valuable and unique, not just because of your race.

I've realized that accepting who I am ethnically and culturally is just as important as accepting myself racially. But I've also found it vastly more difficult, because that's the part of me that people interact with and by which they make judgments about whether I am "this" or "that." And I'm pretty sure that's what most do—after they hear that I am black and white, they evaluate my mannerisms, language, clothing and probably a dozen other things, trying to determine which one I *really* am, rather than seeing and relating to me as a whole person. This seems to be the human way, and we all do it to each other.

We have to accept that we were raised with certain values; taught (or not taught) to observe certain customs and celebrations; taught (or not taught) certain languages and corporate history. Growing up, we lived in communities where we either saw reflections of ourselves or didn't. There we picked up certain cultural cues and ways of being that influence who we are right now.

Both good values and bad exist in every cultural system and thus in *us*. Many ethnic and cultural characteristics are simply neutral—neither good nor bad. I am learning how to say, "By the grace of God I am what I am" (1 Cor 15:10).

Decide who you want to become. As children and adolescents, we don't have much control over the forces that shape us. Once we leave the home of our parents, however, we have much more freedom to choose where and how we will live, who we will relate to, what we will expose ourselves to and what we will learn.

Those of us who ethnically belong to a certain people group but for whatever reason have not been exposed to the cultural values and practices of this community can eventually learn and then live in the fullness of the cultural realities of our ethnic heritage. Even if we weren't raised to do so, we can choose to do so now—particularly if we immerse ourselves in a community where we can gain a sense of cultural kinship with others.

In a study of black-Japanese people, Christine Iijima Hall found that "most of her subjects went through a process of choosing an ethnic identity between the ages of fourteen and eighteen. Over half of them chose to regard themselves as Black Americans, lived in Black neighborhoods, spoke Black English, and had predominantly Black friends.

Some had to work at achieving a Black identity. For instance, those who had spent much of their childhood in Japan could not speak Black English and had to 'learn . . . how to be black' as teenagers in America" (Spickard, pp. 149-50). The salient point here is that it *was* possible for them to learn how to be black. They found acceptance among blacks more readily than other groups—so blackness became, at least publicly, the whole of their identity.

Moses: A Multicultural Brother

Moses, the great prophet and leader of the ancient Israelites, is a good example of learning ethnicity. He was ethnically an Israelite. The Israelites were descended from Noah's son Shem (where we get the title "Semite") after the great flood (Gen 11:10-26). Because of the events occurring shortly after Moses' birth, however, he was put in a situation where he was raised to be culturally Egyptian (Ex 1:22—2:6).

God worked it out that Moses' Israelite mother could nurse him (Ex 2:8). This gave him the chance to be exposed to his Israelite ethnicity at least for his first couple of years. But after that he had little to no exposure to Hebrew culture, as far as we can tell. His family was Egyptian. He lived in the pharaoh's palace. The pharaoh's daughter "adopted him and brought him up as her own son" (Acts 7:21). He was "instructed in all the wisdom of the Egyptians" (Acts 7:22), and all the treasures of Egypt would have been his if he had not left (Heb 11:26).

However, "when he was forty years old, it came into his heart to visit his relatives, the Israelites" (Acts 7:23). After thirty-eight or so years of Egyptian acculturation, it finally clicked for Moses that his ethnic group by birth, the people group from which he descended, were the ones being oppressed all around him by his adoptive pharaoh grandfather. The university grad who had made it out finally went back to the "hood." An affinity for his people, who were in grave condition, rose up in his heart.

Moses was angry about their situation and showed his anger by killing an Egyptian. His Israelite kin, however, were not impressed and did not give any indication that they saw him as one of their own. Moses fled, and for another forty years he lived in yet another culture, that of

Midian (current-day Saudi Arabia). When he first arrived there, he was called an Egyptian, indicating how culturally Egyptian he was, perhaps in his language, dress and customs.

At the age of eighty, he had still not connected culturally with his Israelite roots. For this to happen, God had to call Moses to go and bring the Israelites out of slavery in Egypt. When God first gave him his assignment, Moses resisted hard, saying he couldn't do it and that the Israelites wouldn't follow him. Surely he remembered what had happened forty years earlier when he had tried to show his loyalty to his people—they had rejected him. He also told God he was slow of speech, perhaps partially referring to his inability to speak the Israelites' Hebrew language. God appointed his brother Aaron, specifically described as a Jewish descendant ("Levite") who spoke "fluently," to speak to the people on Moses' behalf (Ex 4:16).

Moses eventually aligned himself fully with his Israelite brothers and sisters, leading them out of slavery and for forty years through the wilderness, where God formed them and gave the commandments and commemorations that actually made them a community. When Moses died at the age of 120, the Israelites wept for him (Deut 34:8). It was said that there had never been a prophet like Moses in all of Israel, nor would there be until Jesus, whom Moses foreshadowed.

The story of Moses encourages us that it is possible to develop an identity that fully reflects our ethnicity regardless of how we were raised. But it warns us as well: this development will require suffering and risk-taking. Learning a language others assume you should know makes you vulnerable. Presenting yourself as a group member when you look or sound different and have some different experiences creates tension. Caring about the causes of your people will require you to be inconvenienced and uncomfortable; it will hurt your heart.

Alexis Spencer-Byers has wanted to visit a local Chinese church for a while now. But it feels very risky. "I'm torn—I want to go, I want to discover the Chinese Christian community. But there's a fear . . . that I'm going to realize it's a crosscultural experience. I want to find my roots, but I'm going to feel unrooted. I'm scared that it'll feel worse than not going. . . . I'm scared of what I will find out." She says it would be easier to visit a Greek Orthodox church—it's *supposed* to be crosscultural.

Alexis yearns to find family but knows that she might be treated as an outsider. Yet the only way to know is to go. The only way to find commonality is to build friendships. And where differences are found instead, that's to be expected.

We should expect cultural diversity within racial and ethnic groups depending on socioeconomic factors, education, religious beliefs, regional differences and the like. Even monoracial people at times find themselves in crosscultural situations with people of their own race. So regardless of what aspects of Chinese culture Alexis finds at the Chinese church, it won't negate the fact that she *is* Chinese. Immersing herself in situations like the church is the only way to experience aspects of her ethnicity that she hasn't yet known.

Some Things I've Learned About Being Many in One

As I have traveled toward a fully biracial identity, I've learned to embrace how I am similar to *and* different from those in my racial groups. I am more like my black friends in some things, more like my white friends in others—and this is OK.

I've also realized that the similarities I share with people often don't have anything to do with race. Americans far too quickly racialize characteristics and preferences. My black uncle, who lives in the heart of an urban area, periodically retreats to a remote lake and enjoys boating and fishing in solitude. He's said he sometimes thinks about moving to the mountains to live in a cabin. These diversions and desires are not often associated with blacks in urban America. Just as no race has exclusive rights to certain facial features, no race has exclusive rights to particular pastimes or personality traits.

I have learned that being both black and white in one person has made me a third type of person who is different in a sense from either blacks or whites. I haven't had the same experience as a white person with two white parents or as a black person with two black parents, though there are some similarities in both cases. Again, *this is OK.*

I have reached a point of accepting that I am more than the sum of my parts. I am not better than my parts, nor do I transcend them. I am definitely a combination of them. But this combination gives me a certain perspective that is unique to a descendant of more than one racial and ethnic group. I recognize good and bad in both groups. (Monoracial people can do this as well, but not as members of both groups.) I feel an affinity for and loyalty to members of both, and it tears me apart to see them at odds with one another.

I bawled at the movie *Rosewood* because it reminded me how greatly blacks, including my family, have been violated in our country. My tears, however, were not only for the injustice but also for the division. I've seen monoracial people be content with the separation between races in a way that many multiracial people can't be. Most biracial people I know are least comfortable in settings that are all one race or the other, because in these situations they most acutely feel how they are different from others in their racial groups.

I have learned that as long as racial groups remain mostly segregated, I need to keep entering black social circles and not avoid people because I'm afraid of rejection. If I give in to fear or intimidation, others may read my hesitance as a message that I don't want to be with them. My fear will become a self-fulfilling prophecy. On the other hand, if I communicate, "I want to be with you," usually people will say, "Come on in!"

I cannot deny either of my people groups, because they both contribute to who I am. I will always see the world as a black-white person, someone who is constantly yearning for the two sides of myself, internally and externally, to embrace one another as long-lost relatives.

Multiple Choice

You can't change your identity, but you can change how you identify. Accept who you are and then be who you want to be. *Don't* live as an apology! And don't feel responsible for others' discomfort with or dislike of your choices.

You can choose to identify with all of your ethnic groups. You can be both/and. You don't have to give in to the pressure to pick one. A Japanese-Jewish American woman was told by an activist friend, "You must decide if you are yellow, or if you are white. Are you part of the

Third World, or are you against it?"

She says, "I laughed at his question. How could I possibly be one and not the other? I was born half-yellow and half-white. I could not be one and not the other anymore than I could cut myself in half and still exist as a human being" (Spickard, p. 117).

Your racial and ethnic identity is not the same thing as your political identity. This man's linking of "yellow" and "Third World" (or of "white" and being "against it") is highly presumptuous and reductionistic. You can have a biracial identity and still be on the side of justice. You can say you're both and not be in favor of white, Western world domination.

Another choice you can make is to emphasize one ethnicity over the other(s), though you need to be careful not to degrade the part of you that you put aside, whether temporarily or permanently. Someone I met at a multiracial people's conference shared with me afterward, "I can decide what I want to identify as. Multiracial in some settings, African American in others. Never white really. That doesn't work for me. And that can change too. But it is up to me and not the person asking me, 'What are you?'" Ethnic identity is not static, and others cannot tell you what yours is.

You can even adopt an ethnic identity that perhaps isn't yours by birth—as Moses most likely did when he lived in Midian for forty years and married a Midianite woman. Or as missionaries often do, based on Paul's saying that he was a "Jew to the Jews" and a "Greek to the Greeks."

A Japanese-white biracial young man told me that because his social circle at school is predominantly black, he thinks of himself as one-third white, one-third Asian and a one-third mix of different things, including black. Because of who his friends are and how he dresses he was once asked, "Are you 'Jason Kidd' black?"[1] Of course, because ethnicity is deeply personal and highly significant to people, we shouldn't make this choice lightly or on a whim ("That bulgogi I had the other night was really good. I think I'll be Korean.").

Some might choose to embrace an identity based on not fitting in or

---

[1]Jason Kidd is a light-skinned black man who plays in the National Basketball Association.

on being different. Ironically, the identity of not belonging provides a way to belong, in that one can connect with others who have chosen the same identity. One biracial friend wrote to me, "In my family, there was a strong sense of acceptance for being different (as if 'different' were normal, if that makes sense). . . . Knowing that one is unique (though it can be painful at times) can be a point of celebration, once accepted."

Psychologist Beverly Daniel Tatum suggests, "What is most significant for the children of interracial unions ultimately is not what label they claim, but the self-acceptance they have of their multiracial heritage" (Tatum, p. 186). Whatever we choose should engender our wholeness and move us toward our purpose. It should also take into consideration that each of us has a responsibility to our fellow human beings. Many of us need to get educated about how racism and injustice continue to affect people's lives, and then commit ourselves to fighting with them, as Moses did. He didn't regain Hebrew culture simply for the sake of being more "ethnic," but in the process of struggling for the freedom of his people who had been enslaved for four hundred years.

While it is difficult to develop an integrated sense of self, it is not impossible, particularly since we have a God who is committed to our wholeness, who teaches us truths that we don't hear in the world. God knows the reasons for our existence as multiracial and multiethnic people and can give us each the sense of acceptance and destiny we need in order to enjoy how we've been made and who we're becoming.

For Reflection and Action

Are you happy with who you are ethnically? As you work out your ethnic identity, think about or do the following:

☐ What values and cultural traits has your family passed on to you, perhaps even nonexplicitly?

☐ Are you ashamed of any racial or ethnic parts of yourself? How is racism (your own or others') affecting your identity?

☐ Expose yourself to or even immerse yourself in one of your cultures. For example, join a church or community organization, move to a different neighborhood, or visit the country of your relatives or ancestors. Learning about where we come from provides a rootedness that many of us (including monoracial people) are lacking.

☐ Learn some of one (or more) of your peoples' languages.

☐ There are a growing number of campus and community groups you can join if you're interested in talking with others who are developing a multiracial and multiethnic identity (see appendix three).

☐ If you feel most comfortable identifying solely with one ethnic community, that is your right. But if even a small part of you wonders about how being part Scandinavian or part Korean or part *whatever* affects you, don't be afraid to explore it. Neither your exploration nor your discoveries will make you any less what you were before—only more yourself.

Along the way to multiethnic wholeness, we want and need friends who will take time to understand us and be with us in our self-discovery process. My friend Melissa, who is a biethnic and bicultural Latina, expresses this need in her poem "Quiero que me entiendas."

Quiero que me entiendas

Aquí and here.
And I have to start here because I know
that this is the only place I can make myself understood.
Pero quiero usar esto para expresar
who I am
Aquí.

Soy en ambos pero without being in either
Y no me gusta,
pero aquí
(or here?)
yo soy.

And how do I expect to be able to tell you
where I am
without knowing myself?
All the same, I beg you to follow,
con paciencia,
follow me
Here y aquí.

I Want You to Understand Me

Here and here
And I have to start here because I know
that this is the only place I can make myself understood.
But I want to use this to express
who I am
Here.

I'm in both but without being in either
And I don't like it,
But here,
(or here?)
I am.

And how do I expect to be able to tell you
where I am
without knowing myself?
All the same, I beg you to follow,
with patience,
follow me
Here and here.[2]

—MELISSA CAMACHO

---

[2]Melissa Camacho was born in New York City and raised in Southern California by her first generation Peruvian mother and first generation Colombian father. She wrote this poem during a period when she was frustrated with not being understood on her majority-white campus, but even more frustrated with not knowing how to make herself understood. Reading Lorna Dee Cervantes, a Chicana poet, inspired her to write her own poem.

4

Our Core Identity

I sat against the brick wall. Beneath me, the cement's coldness penetrated my bones. It was all I could think about at first. Then slowly my mind came around to the assignment. "What does it mean that God is my Father? What does it mean to be a daughter of God?"

I was one of several staff members for a large Christian fellowship at UCLA. We were on our back-to-school retreat. The student leaders had presented the year's vision statement, part of which was "Being Daughters and Sons of God." Now we were reflecting on how we could individually live the vision out.

I have a love-hate relationship with "reflection times." On the one hand, they almost always bring helpful self-knowledge. They even occasionally bring reality-shifting revelations. They help you hear from God. On the other hand, they also always involve restlessness, aggravating mental wandering, and so many thoughts about the futility of trying to listen to God that it hardly feels worth it to make yourself sit down and do it.

But there I was, sitting down and doing it because everyone else was. I repeated the assigned question over and over to myself. The realization set in, like the cold hardness under me, that I had no idea how to answer the question "What does it mean to be a son or daughter of God?" Sure, I could come up with something pat (like "He loves me") and use the rest of my reflection time finding and eating the leftover potato chips from last night's snack time. Instead I grew increasingly troubled as I searched within myself for a more significant answer.

Not to God's surprise, I'm sure, I could not come up with one.

So I decided to ask God. If he was the parent, he should have a good answer. "God, what does it mean that you're my Father?"

As in most cases when I ask God a question, I was not expecting that an answer would come right then. I probably only half-believed God heard me. I sat back against the wall, wishing the exercise were over because I had no idea how to arrive at a satisfying answer for this most basic of questions. (*Where* were those potato chips?)

Not more than three seconds after I had asked the question (about God being my father, not about the chips), an Asian father and son, walking hand in hand, came around the corner of the church where I sat. The little boy toddled slowly, and the father minced his steps to accommodate. Two feet past me, the boy pulled his hand away and stepped into the bushes between the sidewalk where I sat and the parking lot. He stood with his arms tight against his sides, eyes averted, as if trying to make himself disappear.

The father spoke gently in a language I couldn't understand. I didn't need to understand to hear God answering my question, for next the man bent down, picked up his son and held him tightly. The boy relaxed in his arms. He didn't protest. He didn't scream or kick. He went willingly to the preschool at the end of the church building—because his daddy was taking him. He didn't want to go, but he went because his daddy went with him.

"This is what it means that I am your Father and you are my daughter" registered in my mind. I was still stunned by the touching drama that had just unfolded before my eyes. God kept talking. "I am with you always. And when there are places that you don't want to go because you are afraid, I will assure you with my love; I will pick you up and carry you there,"

God took me to the book of Deuteronomy and showed me this: "The LORD your God, who goes before you, is the one who will fight for you, just as he did for you in Egypt before your very eyes, and in the wilderness, where you saw how the LORD your God carried you, just as one carries a child, all the way that you traveled until you reached this place" (Deut 1:30-31). What I had just seen and heard was right there—in the Bible! God had spoken to me.

A beloved son or daughter of God—conformed to the obedient Son Jesus, who went with his Father wherever he took him—is who God wants us to be. When we become Christians, that becomes our primary identity.

Children by Grace, Not by Race

As multiracial people we may have asserted that we don't want to choose—"we are not *either* this *or* that." But then we are left asking, "So what does it mean to be both/and?" How do I have a racial identity that according to the society around me does not exist? is not affirmed? cannot be? an identity that is hard to find a model of—even in my own home, where each of my parents gives me a piece of who I am but is not exactly who I am? *Who am I?*

If we want to know who we are, asking the One who made us is a good place to start. We need to let God orient our identity. Otherwise we will be ensnared in human-made constructs and others' definitions of who we are (or who they think we should be) that have little or nothing to do with reality.

As I've walked with God, I've gained a conviction from his Word about the beginning and ending of who we are. God's very first words about us tell us of our core identity: "Let us make humankind in our image, according to our likeness" (Gen 1:26). Our identity is found in reflecting God, who is three persons in one being (very much like us multiracial and multiethnic people)!

Being made according to the likeness of the triune God is the deep well from which we draw to know who we are. We are made with the capacity to love, create, communicate, rule and do a hundred other things God the Father does. We are to be joyful, humble servants and a hundred other things God the Son is. We can comfort, encourage and speak truth, similar to God the Spirit. God, by his grace, made us to be like him. This is the identity he wants us to be pursuing.

We are God's image bearers. God's image in us, however, is severely distorted because of choices we have made to establish ourselves as our own gods. We were never meant to rule ourselves. But God doesn't give up on us.

Romans 8:28 says, "We know that all things work together for good for those who love God, who are called according to his purpose." This might be a familiar passage to you, but did you realize that in context this verse talks about your identity? Verse 29 reads "For those whom he foreknew he also predestined to be conformed to the image of his Son, in order that he [Jesus] might be the firstborn within a large family." God's purpose for us—the good end to which all things are working together—is that we would be reformed and conformed to the likeness of Jesus, and that together we'd be one family under God.

Jesus is central in God's plan. That's because he is God in the flesh, the image of God (2 Cor 4:4)—the most tangible way we can see who God is and know him personally. He is the One in whose image we are being remade since we compromised God's image in us. Among Jesus' many characteristics, one lies at the core of his identity. God announces this when he says, "This is my Son, the Beloved, with whom I am well pleased" (Mt 3:17).

Being God's beloved Son is central to Jesus' identity. If one of God's primary goals is to remake us like Jesus, then being God's beloved children should be central to our identity too. Most of our problems proceed from not holding on to this primary identity of "Beloved." Scripture helps us know and remember who we are, though.

> It is no longer I who live, but it is *Christ who lives in me.* And the life I now live in the flesh I live by faith in the Son of God, *who loved me and gave himself for me.* (Gal 2:20, emphasis added)

> For you have died, and *your life is hidden with Christ in God. . . .* You have stripped off the old self with its practices and have clothed your-

selves with the new self, which is being renewed in knowledge *according to the image of its creator.* In that renewal there is no longer Greek and Jew, circumcised and uncircumcised, barbarian, Scythian, slave and free; but Christ is all and in all! (Col 3:3, 9-11, emphasis added)

For in Christ Jesus you are all *children of God* through faith. As many of you as were baptized into Christ have *clothed yourselves with Christ.* There is no longer Jew or Greek, there is no longer slave or free, there is no longer male and female; for all of you are one in Christ Jesus. (Gal 3:26-28, emphasis added)

In this paradigm racial, ethnic and cultural identities are subordinate to our identity as image-bearers and loved children of God. And when we accept this primary personal identity from God, our primary corporate identity becomes belonging to the new "large family" (Rom 8:29) that God is creating, where all are one in Christ Jesus. Our primary corporate identity is no longer attached to certain racial groups.

God's reality has been freeing for me—someone who has more often obsessed about my racial identity than ignored it. I am first and foremost Sundee, the beloved daughter of God who is daily being made to reflect the image of my Creator. I have clothed myself with Christ, and it is most important that people see him when they look at me—not that they see a black woman or a white woman. Christ lives in me. God, in taking on human flesh, dignified *all* human flesh, regardless of its color.

For Matt McDonell, son of a Mexican-American mother and an Irish-American father, knowing that he is first of all God's son helps a lot. "It makes the fuzziness of being biracial less daunting or scary, to know that it's not the ultimate source of my identity, but just one of the aspects that shape the way I come to understand and apply different truths.

"With Christianity as my starting place, and not my race, . . . I feel free to step outside the traditions and values of my culture when they are challenged by a truth of the gospel without feeling that I'm being untrue to who I am. The gospel ultimately defines who I am."

David Gibbons, pastor of a multiethnic church in Orange County,

California, wrestled all his life with the question *Why did God make me this way—externally Asian, but internally American and Western?* As a kid growing up in a predominantly white and Hispanic Arizona town, he was called Chink and Chinaman. People slanted their eyes at him, whispered behind his back and asked him questions like "Can you see through your eyes when you smile?" Even friends asked these things.

The fact that his dad was white didn't make any difference. To the non-Asian people around him he looked Asian, and he was treated as such.

Dave's urge to fight back and to defend himself slowly turned into a ravenous desire to be accepted. "I wanted to blend in as much as possible. I wanted to be known as one of them, not part of the immigrant community with their strange accents and awkwardness. I was fixed on excelling in the white community and bent on avoiding Asians and Asian culture because of embarrassment."

He joined the football team and became known as a leader. He asked his white high school friends, "Do you see me as any different?" And they'd say, "No, why are you even asking?" Dave had achieved his goal, but at the cost of his wholeness. Underneath this successful leader's skin, self-hatred had taken root. He viewed himself as unattractive and not good enough. He was still ashamed of being Asian.

Much later in his life, in a graduate seminary class, Dave heard a lecture on who we are in Christ. Afterward God caused the message finally to sink in. "It hit me: I'm God's son! It filled my cup. The quest for whether I was Asian or Western, Korean or American, became irrelevant in the sense that I didn't gain value from it. I finally saw my position in Christ. My wife saw the difference. Once I was more secure it freed me to explore my culture more."

We are God's beloved ones because Jesus lives in us and he is *the* Beloved One. We are now daughters and sons of God because he is *the* Son of God, and we are brothers and sisters of one another irrespective of ethnicity. We are children of God by grace, not by race.

So Can We Forget About Race?

In this world no one is race-free. "The criteria that people use for race are based entirely on external features that we are programmed to recognize," says Dr. Douglas C. Wallace, professor of molecular genetics at Emory University School of Medicine in Atlanta. "And the reason we're programmed to recognize them is that it's vitally important to our species that each of us be able to distinguish one individual from the next" (Angier). We cannot escape people's need to classify racial differences or the social construct of race, even if we know its biological premise is faulty.[1] Likewise, everyone has an ethnicity—it's the way God has made us. We do not relinquish all ethnic ties, nor do our ethnic identities become invalid, when we become Christians. If you think you have no ethnicity or that your ethnicity is not important now that you belong to "the race of God's people," not so. If you haven't made any intentional decisions about your ethnic identity, you are most likely a product of whatever culture dominates in your home, school and friendships (not necessarily a bad thing, just the reality).

Ethnos is the Greek word from which we get *ethnicity*, and it appears over and over in the Bible. One place it appears is Revelation 7, where the author John describes representatives from every ethnos worshiping Jesus. God made ethnicity and it's here to stay, even throughout eternity according to the biblical picture.

When I asked God what it meant that he was my Father, he sent me a powerful lesson about my need to let him conform me into the likeness of Jesus, the Beloved Son who went wherever his Father took him. My primary identity was to be a beloved child who would willingly allow God to carry me.

There was another message God had for me, however—one about ethnic identity.

God had spoken to me through an Asian father carrying his son to a dreaded preschool. Another reflection time begun in great disquietude had ended in awe and worship. I had to tell the UCLA group about it. I left my finally warm cement spot and went inside.

I told my story, and our meeting went on as usual. Except for Andrew. He was a student I'd known for two years. He struggled

---

[1]For more on the scientific versus social underpinnings of race, see appendix one.

greatly with his personal identity. At the root of it all, of course, was his struggle to know himself as God's beloved son.

He came up to me now, distress written all over his face. "Can we talk?" he whispered.

We went into a side room. The story had moved Andrew, especially the fact that the father and son were Asian. It had obviously agitated and upset him as well.

Andrew was born in Taiwan but moved to the States when he was very young. Culturally, he had adapted to his white American surroundings. Now he said, "I don't think God can relate to me as an Asian. I think my Asian friends can understand me better than God." In the process of adaptation, Andrew had adopted a white concept of God.

I could see why Andrew would be distressed. How could he put his trust in a God who had no clue about something so deeply at the core of who he was? How could he be the beloved son of someone he believed was culturally foreign? How could he be close to a Father who couldn't speak his language, literally or metaphorically?

Of course God can speak Mandarin, French, Russian, Spanish, Swahili and every other language known on the face of the earth. God can speak into the heart of any person of any ethnicity and make himself known as the Creator of that person, including the features that grace her face, the beautiful color of her skin or the culturally influenced impulses that are ingrained in her heart. It's often hard, however, for us to appropriate this for ourselves, to grasp that these facets of our ethnicity are also reflections of God's image.

I assured Andrew that God knew him deeply, including his ethnicity. God is the ultimate source of ethnicity—not our earthly mothers and fathers.

Then I marveled over the largeness of God and his attentiveness to his beloved bicultural son, as Andrew poured out his heart in Mandarin to his "Baba." I had no doubt that God understood every word that Andrew prayed. Or that God cared greatly about Andrew's ethnicity and knew how it informed this young man's sense of self. God is the Father of all people of every ethnicity.

Clearly my friend Andrew's ethnicity was important to God. I think God intentionally had me see an Asian father and son because he had something to say to Andrew as well as to me.

Ethnicity is important because through our variety we testify to the creative imagination and power of God. The fact that God made Andrew a Taiwanese American caused my own understanding of God to be enlarged. (God is *not* white, as we are prone to conceptualize him in the West, and he *does* speak Mandarin.) The fact that we are created in all our ethnic differentness gives us more cause to praise the Creator.

I believe God couldn't help but create diversity—he's too grand for his image to be reflected by just one ethnicity. In fact, he's so vast and multifaceted that his creativity expands beyond the racial categories humans have established. He makes combinations in single individuals that according to society are scandalous, outrageous, impossible. Yes, he is *that* creative and unwilling to be boxed in by people's limited perspectives on what's right and wrong, what's "natural."

God embeds our ethnicity deep in our soul. It is an important part of how we reflect his glory. We don't have to (and ought not) throw it out when we accept God's invitation to become one of his children. We must accept, however, that though God loves the ethnicity he's made us, it is not ethnicity that causes him to love. We must let him put our race and ethnicity into perspective.

Some of us have made race and ethnicity too important. We obsess over our racial identity until it looms larger in our lives than God does. We make decisions primarily influenced by race and not God's values. Or we cling to ethnicity as our primary source of identity and can't imagine who we'd be without it. When we do this we make race and ethnicity an idol.

Others of us have ignored various ethnic parts of ourselves, feeling that they create too much conflict. We haven't been able to relate to "being German" or "being Japanese" or "being Lakota," and so we've tried to forget about these parts. But still they keep calling—*because they're a part of who God has made us.* We can ignore them to the point that they eventually shrivel and go into remission, if not die completely. We can deny them the chance ever to inform and enliven our sense of self. Or we can explore them, let them enhance our understanding of God, our world and ourselves, and feast on their richness.

We can be confident that God cares about our ethnicity and relates to us as ethnic individuals. He made us as we are, and no matter what is communicated to us otherwise, the ethnic combination God made in us is *good*. Even if you feel unknowable because your ethnic makeup is unusual, God knows you to the depths of your being. Your ethnicity reflects a part of who God is. You're not foreign to God but came out of God's very imagination. Do you believe that you are a good creation who is known?

Keep your ears and eyes open to God, and he will tell and show you how *he* sees you, which is what you really need.

Letting God Show Us How He Sees Us

A multiethnic conference brought together most of our organization's ethnic minority employees and some white employees as well. The first morning, an Asian American sister spoke. She emphasized that when God spread the message about Jesus beyond his 120 followers to the diverse peoples who had gathered in Jerusalem for Pentecost (a Jewish festival), he did it in their own languages. In other words, he took their cultures seriously.

He could have had Jesus' disciples proclaim his mighty deeds in their native Aramaic—it was the trade language, and most people would have understood it. Instead God caused the 120 Jesus-followers, who couldn't speak these languages, to speak them, proving that he was intimately acquainted with each language and thus each culture. God spoke to flesh through flesh, showing that he didn't and doesn't disdain our humanity, including our ethnicity. By doing it this way, he was saying to each person in the crowd, "I know who you are. I am the God of all nations (and all ethnic groups)." He validated their ethnic and cultural backgrounds.

As soon as the speaker finished, a memory came to my mind. Its relevance was immediately clear. I thought of being in seventh grade, when I first heard about Jesus in a way that made sense and I accepted God's invitation to have a relationship with him. A black woman had told me! God spoke through the flesh of a black woman to deliver his invitation to me.

Here I was, years later, a full-fledged adult, still wondering where I fit racially. I heard him speaking to me again: "I affirm the black in you. That's why I spoke my good news to you through a black woman. So that when you were at this point in your life, still wondering about your identity, torn up with questions about where you belong in the race picture, you would know that I know you're black as well as white. Even if no one else in your color-obsessed world ever sees you that way because of how you look, I do."

Relief, joy and sadness intermingled in my tears as I sat there, realizing that God knew who I was even if no one else did. Even if *I* didn't always know myself. He knew that the African American part of me had been underemphasized in my life. He was helping me claim it as a part of me—helping me put the puzzle of my racial identity together.

In case you're wondering, I'm not saying that if you first heard from God through a Korean American woman and you are a Latino-white man, it means God sees you as a Korean American woman. This was a way that he validated a part of *my* ethnicity that needed validating. God will speak differently to you. (Maybe God's speaking to you right now, through the flesh of this *biracial* woman!)

We don't need to choose between being God's beloved children and belonging to our ethnicity. Before we can understand our ethnicity rightly, however, we need to receive and live in the truth that our primary identity is found in being conformed to Jesus' image, in order to reveal him to the world. If we have received the Beloved Son into our lives, we are foremost God's beloved sons and daughters, and his family is the one to which we give primary allegiance.

With these truths in place, we can follow God into a full understanding of who we are, including the ethnicity and culture he's given us. He will cause us to worship him as we see his beauty reflected in the totality of how he's made us. Our ethnicity will be put in proper perspective as a means by which God is magnified.

For Reflection and Action

☐ Have you accepted the truth that you are first and foremost God's "beloved daughter" or "beloved son"? Are you allowing God to carry you where you might not want to go?

☐ Remind yourself daily that you are clothed with Christ, and pursue being like him as your primary identity. Read Matthew, Mark, Luke or John in the Bible and take note of Jesus' traits.

☐ List five things you like about yourself. Thank God for creating you in his image.

☐ How is God re-creating you as you follow him? Pick one characteristic of the triune God that you would like to see developed in you (such as compassion, love of truth, commitment to justice, ability to encourage, being a servant, creativity), and ask God to develop this in you.

☐ Seek out a Christian community where you can experience belonging to the family of God *and* have your ethnic identity encouraged and affirmed.

☐ How has your perception of God been shaped by how and where you were raised? Do you believe God understands and knows who you are, including your ethnicity, and that your ethnic mix reflects something of who God is? (You might try talking to God in your first language if that's not something you usually do.)

☐ Ask God to show you how he sees you.

Reflections on Being a Quarter Chinese

Apologizing to the worker at the blood bank,
> *"Ma'am, I'm sorry, but I'm not white—I'm other."*
Laughing over how my young cousin stated her identity
to our grandmother:
> *"Nai Nai, Nai Nai, guess what?*
> *I'm a nickel Chinese!"*
Trying to eat Uncle Ben's Converted Rice with chopsticks.
Explaining why I don't know how to cook tempura.
Changing my school identity from white to Chinese,
> *only to realize that made it more difficult to get*
into my high school of choice.
Eagerly awaiting the 2000 Census' multi-racial option.
Wearing Chinese slippers with blue jeans.
Answering no to the myriad variations of the question:
> *"Are you Puerto Rican? . . . Greek? . . . Jewish? . . . Italian? . . . Mexican?"*
Identifying with the oppressor and the oppressed, and
then the oppressor again.
(Needing forgiveness from the Japanese—twice.)
Wondering if I should marry a Chinese man so my
children will "count" for the race.
Wondering if I should marry a non-white, non-Chinese
man so they will just be "American."
Realizing that I have family halfway 'round the world
> *whom I've never met*
> *and probably never will*
> *and to whom I couldn't speak if I ever did*
unless they happened to know English . . . or German.
Insisting that just because I'm not half-and-half,
> *that doesn't mean I'm not biracial.*
Knowing that God made me just the way I am,
> *that I'm rich*
> *and special*
> *and a beloved daughter of the King . . .*
and of a white man . . . and of a half-Chinese woman.[2]

—ALEXIS SPENCER-BYERS

---

[2]Alexis Spencer-Byers is a Chinese-white biracial woman whose passions are racial and gender reconciliation, youth ministry and writing (though generally not poetry). The inspiration behind this poem was that I asked for her thoughts about being biracial, and she took the opportunity to jot down some of the joys, frustrations, oddities and issues that accompany being multiracial.

5

Temptations We Face

With each word of the corporate prayer of confession I felt worse. I was at a major national convention, and we were asking for God's forgiveness for the sins of our own racial group. A South African black man and an American white man led us. *If you are white, repent for the white people who oppressed and dehumanized blacks. If you are black, repent for the black people who won't forgive the whites. Sing a song. Hug. Now doesn't that feel better?* I wasn't engaging. I couldn't get past the fact that everyone else only had to repent once, while I had to do it twice. I was definitely getting the raw end of the deal!

A powerful act of contrition and grace-giving had occurred. It was transracial, transcultural, transnational even, and all I could do was sit in my seat and seethe. This was so unfair! Was anyone thinking about the people in the crowd who couldn't be easily categorized? Even though I was smack-dab in the middle of this black and white picture, I felt completely left out.

I squeezed out of the arena with the other eighteen thousand attendees, but I was totally alone. Feeling overwhelmed by the news that I had two races to repent for, I became frantic and started looking for a friend to shoulder this burden with me. Could God really expect this from me? I was being tempted to think God was cruel and callous for making me a both/and person. And I was giving in. This cross was too heavy to bear.

For a multiracial person, it's easy to feel this way. And yet God is perfect in all his ways, and everything he has made is good. "The Rock [God], his work is perfect, and all his ways are just" (Deut 32:4). "This God—his way is perfect; the promise of the LORD proves true; he is a shield for all who take refuge in him" (2 Sam 22:31). "God saw everything that he had made, and indeed, it was very good" (Gen 1:31). When we insist on thinking otherwise, we distance ourselves from God and forfeit the benefits of being close to him.

I clearly needed help to believe God was still good (and had made something good in me) in spite of the fact that I felt awful and oppressed. Instead of finding that help, I meandered outside in the sub-freezing weather, trying to look like I knew where I was going. God had nicely coordinated my external and internal situations, which I find he often does to make his point. My heart was too cold to get it.

Much is unfair about the world. Anyone who takes up residency here will be wronged and do wrong. It is tempting to blame our unfair situations on God, to say that God has messed us over when we are feeling torn by racial and ethnic discord. After all, he's ultimately responsible for making us the way we are. He knew it was going to be hard for us. So why didn't he make us some other way?

Questions like this one can lead to a number of temptations for us as multiracial people. The easiest to see is bitterness.

Bitterness

I was hanging out in a friend's dorm room one night when the issue of being multiracial came up. One of the students had seen a video in class that day on the subject. Sort of. It was a copy of an Oprah Winfrey show, and the guests had been people of multiracial heritage. As I listened, what came across most clearly was that these folks were angry. They were angry at whites who were prejudiced against minorities, and they were angry at minorities who held them suspect because they had "white blood." Caught in the crossfire, they reacted by getting out their own guns and firing both ways.

It struck me then that it would be very easy for us to find reasons to be angry at all the racial groups of which we are made up. There are many historical examples of whites subjugating mixed people as harshly as they would "full-blooded" minorities. We can find examples of ethnic minorities distrusting those who have white lineage or lineage from other ethnic groups. Add to this the personal experiences most of us have had of being misunderstood, mistreated or excluded by the racial groups of which we're a part. There are reasons to be angry.

Anger is not automatically a problem. But bitterness (unresolved anger) is. Jesus says if we refuse to forgive others, we will forgo the benefits of God's forgiveness in our lives (Mt 18:23-35). Anger is good if taken to God, because he can comfort us in our situation and help us to forgive. He can also turn anger into a positive force—a passion to right what is wrong and subvert injustice.

In the United States a hierarchical system of power has developed in which whites are at the top, first men and then women. Men and women of minority groups occupy the third and fourth tiers. In other words, it goes (in a slightly simplified version): white men, white women, men of color, women of color.

Psychologist Maria P. P. Root argues that "racially mixed men and women would occupy the fifth and sixth tiers in this model, respectively, because of the rigidity of the dichotomy between White and non-White. Subsequently, multiracial people experience a 'squeeze' of oppression *as* people of color and *by* people of color" (Root, *Racially Mixed People,* p. 5).

I agree that multiracial people are squeezed. We face discrimination and prejudice from both sides of the fence. This explains the temptation to be bitter. I disagree, however, with the notion that multiracial people are always at the bottom of the hierarchy. And if we think this way we are in danger of giving into a second temptation, which is self-justification.

Self-Justification

When I was first presented with this idea that multiracial people are at the bottom of a racial-gender food chain, my heart wanted to exult in my victim status. I wanted to say "Amen!" because someone was validating my struggles. I felt justified simply in being at the bottom. It meant I was really all right, while everyone above me was condemned for being oppressors.

One of our greatest temptations is to justify ourselves. None of us wants to admit our utterly self-centered nature or our inability to change this nature—if we even see it as problematic. The truth is that self-centeredness has wrecked the world and continues to wreak havoc in our individual, familial and communal lives. We've inherited a mess, and we *each* continue to contribute to the mess. None of us is able to save ourselves from it.

Thank God, he is committed to cleaning up the mess. All we need to do is agree that we've botched things up and we can't make them right without him. We must beware of using the ways we've been discriminated against as fuel for self-justification—for thinking we're less in need of God's cleanup job than others are.

My tendency to self-justify came to the surface one day in a sociology class on biracial families and individuals. Throughout this course I had hung on my professor's every word. I hadn't been exposed to any of the research or much of the history he was presenting. "Tomorrow we're going to talk about the 'color complex,'" he said on this day. "It's not something blacks typically discuss in the presence of whites, because we don't want them to know that we can discriminate on the basis of skin color just like they do."

I sat there smugly, just waiting for him to say it: darker blacks often discriminate against lighter blacks and biracial people because we aren't purebred. He continued, "Generally speaking, this has been a problem of lighter-skinned blacks discriminating against the darker ones."

The jaw of my heart hit the floor of my guts. Shame overshadowed my self-justifying thoughts and spread into my soul.

The next day he explained further. There was the "paper bag test," which was used at black-operated establishments: blacks were admitted only if their skin was lighter than a brown paper bag. Then there was the "color tax" at black fraternities: the darker the skin of your date, the more you had to pay at the party. I sat in class and lamented how "my race" had sinned.

A 1990 study showed that lighter-skinned blacks are better off financially. At that time a dark-skinned person made seventy-two cents for every dollar a light-skinned black earned. The difference is a result of historical racism that gave lighter and biracial people more access to education and more exposure to white society. Sons and daughters of master-slave unions were seen as having more intelligence and potential because of their white lineage and were often given greater opportunities. The economic ramifications of this prejudice are still apparent today.

When I heard the truth about the past, I learned that it's not as simple as saying, "Biracial people are being oppressed at the bottom of the power structure." We have the potential to discriminate as much as anyone else, as history shows. We have some advantages that others don't. We must be careful not to justify ourselves by subtly suggesting we are the oppressed saints and others are the oppressor sinners.

Arrogance
A third temptation is arrogance, especially now that being multiracial is considered chic. Our visages are flashed all over the place to sell clothes, cars, cell phones—you name it. We're the faces of the future, very vogue and of course *always* good-looking. We have the best of both worlds—Anglo features *and* that Coppertone tan everyone covets. It's tempting to take in marketers' messages and have an inflated and false sense of esteem. While it's good and right to accept and like ourselves the way God made us, we need to avoid arrogance.

It's arrogance to think ourselves superior to those "monoracials." I can wear kente or a kilt, claim kinship with Sojourner Truth *and* Abraham Lincoln, and make black-eyed peas or lefse and call them the food of my ancestors. But in this country, so could a lot of "monoracial" people. Having multiple racial heritages does make us rich, but not superior.

Arrogance makes us think that only our cause matters. We become unconcerned about the plight of other oppressed groups. I faced this temptation at a racial reconciliation conference in Jackson, Mississippi. During one session in which all two hundred participants were gathered, one of the conference organizers confessed his error of not working harder to get a Latino speaker for the conference. He was sorry and wanted to publicly ask the small Latino contingency for their forgiveness. There was a sense of contrition among the group that Latinos were constantly being ignored as dialogue focused on black-white relations and, more recently, Asian issues.

My immediate internal reaction to this man's genuine humility and care was *What about the biracial people at this conference? Did you work to get a self-identified biracial person to speak?* I was so caught up in "my people group" and myself that I had no compassion for my Latino brothers and sisters.

Fortunately, God convicted me of this right away, and I was able to repent and ask for his forgiveness. The point of our gathering was not 100 percent equal representation for all. It was learning to love one another and be reconciled across racial lines. Self-importance and fear of being overlooked had obscured my focus momentarily.

There is nothing wrong with wanting to see multiracial issues taken seriously or to have more resources crafted for our particular needs. I gravitate toward anything that promotes interracial relationships (of all kinds), racial reconciliation or multiracial people. I am eager for more resources and am even producing them myself.

The problem occurs when I and my agenda (or my group's agenda) become more important than God's plan and his desire for justice and compassion for all. Or when I disregard the truth that God has said he will not forget us but fill every need and right every wrong.

Opportunism

At the Jackson conference, the organizers actually had thought of multiracial people. A session for "ethnic-specific" groups included one for people of more than one race. This time I didn't have to choose as I had ten years earlier at the urban program in Pasadena. As it happened, it was because the organizers had heard my story that they created a multiracial group. I was asked to lead it.

I awaited the meeting anxiously, wondering if anyone else would dare identify themselves as more than one race. I imagined myself sitting alone in a hotel conference room for the entire session—just me and Jesus talking about how it feels to be multiracial, the "minority among minorities."

But five other people came. During our session, we talked about issues we needed to face up to in ourselves. A Korean-white brother confessed that he struggled with opportunism—a fourth temptation, defined as siding with one race or the other depending on what is most convenient or advantageous at the time. We all nodded in silent acknowledgment that we too had struggled with this.

He got even more specific. "It's easy not to side with whites when there is corporate confession of what white people did in the past," he said. My previous frustrating experience of corporate confession bounded to the front of my mind.

Implied in what he said was that those of us who had a white parent were as much white as we were black, Chinese, Puerto Rican or Korean. If we were totally honest, we needed to ask God for forgiveness for our white ancestors' racial sins.[1] What our brother said was hard but true.

Another form opportunism might take is choosing to be a minority when it will benefit us academically, financially or socially, but not aligning ourselves with our minority brothers and sisters when it comes to toppling inequitable and unjust systems. "I'm black when it comes to applying for scholarships and employment, but once I get into that school or that job I'm not concerned about racist policies and practices I see" doesn't have integrity. Affirmative action may be dying out (or getting killed out), but as long as it's around and we are benefiting from it we need to work alongside other ethnic minorities for real change.

We also give in to opportunism when we let people think we're

---

[1]The Bible gives many examples of asking God's forgiveness on behalf of one's people. Moses, Ezra, Nehemiah, Job, Daniel and Stephen all did this. (See Neh 1:6-7 for one example.)

someone we're not and don't speak up against racism against our people or others. Because our features often obscure our identity, we sometimes overhear comments that would never be made in the presence of an obvious ethnic minority. Even those who do know us might think of us differently from the way they see "full-blooded" minorities, and might make prejudiced statements, perhaps that they don't realize are prejudiced.

I learned the hard way that it is easy to succumb to the temptation to remain silent. I was standing in my university's registration line. Two white men and a white woman stood in front of me. One of the guys told the other to go out to his car and get something for him. Without missing a beat, the woman retorted, "Does he look black to you?" clearly implying that blacks are subservient to whites and are the only ones who deserve to be ordered around.

I was stunned. I reveal my naiveté by telling you I couldn't believe anyone would say something like this in the year 1990. Anger flared under my skin too pale to tell the truth. *I* was black. But I didn't look it. And so this woman felt free to say what she never would have if a darker person had been standing near her in the line.

Fortunately, one of the men gave her a look that communicated "That wasn't funny," and her brazen laugh turned into insecure tittering before she shut up completely. I fumed but couldn't bring myself to tell her that her "joke" offended me. It felt too awkward.

It is hard for me to admit my silence that day. But through that experience I was confronted with the pernicious presence of racism even among my peers (it's not just a problem among old folks). While it's not one person's sole responsibility to eradicate racism, silence allows racism to be perpetuated. Only God can convict people of their wrong attitudes, but our voices are meant to be some of the instruments through which conviction comes.

Shame

Succumbing to shame about who we are is a fifth temptation. We do not need to give in to cultural and societal pressures to deny parts of ourselves but can affirm the good things that God has created in all races.

Lee was black. His black mother raised him in a black community. Lee's father had never been around. His brother, who had a different father, was black. All of Lee's friends were black. Yet Lee felt different because he looked different. He had light skin, and his eyes didn't look like everyone else's.

One day his mother told Lee a secret. His father was Chinese, but they were not going to tell anyone.

Lee had found the answer he was looking for, but now he was in an even worse dilemma. He couldn't explore his Asian heritage because his mother didn't want people to know. A cloud of shame surrounded Lee's true identity. It wasn't until he was an adult that he began to live free from this shame and to enjoy all of who he was (*Domino*, directed by Shanti Thakur).

After World War II, many soldiers returned to the United States with Japanese brides. History professor Paul R. Spickard describes the pressures even the Japanese mothers would put on their children to be American (read: "white"). Sachiko Pfeiffer is just one example.

> Most of the parents chose to raise their children as Americans. They gave them English names, spoke to them mainly or exclusively in English, and chose American child-rearing practices over the more relaxed Japanese methods. Sachiko Pfeiffer expected to remain in America and to have her children grow up as Americans, marry Americans, and raise American grandchildren. (Spickard, p. 147)

In an attempt to secure acceptance and success in a new country, parents sought to suppress a significant part of these children's ethnic heritage and identity.

Some Japanese who had lived in the United States or Canada for years before the war played down their cultural differences after the trauma of being moved to internment camps. The camps and the anti-Japanese sentiment during this period stated unmistakably that being Japanese was bad, something to be ashamed of.

Margaret's mother was born in a Canadian internment camp. She grew up and married her college sweetheart, a white man. Later Margaret was born. Cultural differences were de-emphasized so much in Margaret's family that she didn't realize her parents were an interracial couple until she was sixteen. Now a college student, she cries as she describes the frustration of not knowing the culture, the music and the stories of her Japanese side. She feels it is wrong that she has to go out and learn this culture that she should have grown up with as a child. These traditions had been stripped away in the internment camps and replaced with shame *(Domino)*.

I've heard it said that shame—the feeling that who you are is wrong—cannot be repented of. This is partially true. We certainly can't repent of ourselves, because we are who we are. Thankfully, we don't need to repent of ourselves, because who we are is good. God says in his Word that we are awesomely and wonderfully made (Ps 139:14). However, if we are deliberately suppressing or despising part of who we are, we are not believing God's Word. We are saying that his craftsmanship is shoddy. We are likely giving in to the standards of the world around us regarding who and what is valuable. These actions we most certainly can repent of.

Finding Hope

Of course reversing our thought patterns is not an easy thing to do. Nor is turning from bitterness, self-justification, arrogance or opportunism. I know this well from firsthand experience. It's hard to give up these sins and instead forgive, trust in God alone for our justification, be humble and follow Jesus rather than our convenience-centered desires. No matter how much I tell myself it shouldn't be, for hard-core fallen human beings like me it's extremely difficult to love God, others and myself.

However, we have a hope. It is our only hope. Thankfully, it's not the one-in-a-million-chance kind of hope. It's not Luke Skywalker versus the Death Star. We don't have to wonder, with breath sucked in and adrenaline racing, *Who's going to emerge victorious—us or these vermin sins?*

Being rooted in God's passionate love is our hope. It's a sure hope, because God has promised that he passionately loves us ("I have loved you with an everlasting love," Jer 31:3), and God never breaks a promise ("God is not a human being, that he should lie, or a mortal, that he should change his mind. Has he promised, and will he not do it?" Num 23:19). God can convince even the most stubborn of his love, because his love for us is stronger than our failures toward him ("He does not deal with us according to our sins, nor repay us according to our iniquities. For as the heavens are high above the earth, so great is his steadfast love toward those who fear him; as far as the east is from the west, so far he removes our transgressions from us," Ps 103:10-12).

When we know God's passionate love, we can admit our failures and shortcomings without the fear of being jilted. When we know his passionate love, none of the temptations in this chapter are that tempting anymore.

Love Covers a Multitude of Sins

My experience of corporate confession at the huge convention that I mentioned earlier brought to the surface an already percolating internal conflict. I felt angry at God for making me the way he had and angry at others for their seeming oversight. I felt sad about the history of sin between the races. I felt the longstanding war between two people groups raging inside myself. I didn't feel God's passionate love.

The temptation was to let these feelings overtake me and to spend the rest of the conference bitter at God and others. Or to feel victimized and therefore justified. Or to stuff my feelings and not give another thought to what God wanted me to do in, or learn from, the situation.

As I roamed the grounds around the conference arena, letting frostbite have my fingers, Jesus wouldn't let frostbite have my heart. I went back inside to look for help.

I found two friends who listened as I spewed my tension, frustration and confusion. I cried and I questioned. I needed to know where God was in all of this. As we prayed, one of them thanked Jesus for being a God who could relate to me in everything that I was feeling. My heart thawed as I was reminded that somehow Jesus would make sense of all this.

Though I don't remember many specifics from the prayers prayed that day, I learned an important lesson. We need our friends' help to deal with the temptations we face and the feelings we have. Don't be afraid to go to your friends and open up your struggles related to being multiracial. This is a core part of who you are, and true friends will want to listen and will treat what you share with sensitivity, even if they don't have all the answers.

Also, don't assume that your nonmultiracial friends won't be able to empathize or have helpful insights for you. Once I lamented to my African American friend Sacha that I am the least black-looking black person I ever knew. She pointed out an advantage that I have over her. As a biracial person with a white parent, I haven't had to work through the deeply entrenched distrust and bitterness toward whites that she dealt with.

It wasn't the response I expected, but it made me think. It increased my gratefulness when I was having a hard time being grateful.

Most of all, we need Jesus' help. Like my friend said in his prayer, Jesus really can relate to us in everything we are feeling and experiencing. Like us, he was never completely understood by those around him. He too lived in an in-between place: He was a human being and God. He bore within himself the conflict between God and people, and he carried that burden all the way to the cross—for us—so a truce could be made.

Have you ever thought that only another biracial person of your same ethnic makeup could understand what you've been through? Jesus understands even more, because he lived with the same tensions as you while he was on earth. Not only that, he has known you and been with you since before you were born (Jer 1:5), experiencing everything that you experience right along with you. No one else can make that claim.

Being multiracial is a fundamental part of who you are. How could Jesus not care about your multiracial experience and your feelings about it? When you love someone passionately, everything that concerns that person concerns you. Jesus loves *you* passionately; therefore everything that concerns *you* concerns *him*.

God isn't a sadist. He doesn't enjoy seeing us suffering or in pain. Nor does he cavalierly allow hardships in our lives as if his only concern were the growth of our character and "toughening us up." When we suffer, he knows about it and he *feels* it. Hebrews 4:15 says that Jesus is able to sympathize with our weaknesses; he is touched by the feelings of our infirmities, because he was tempted in every way we are.

As you face your wrongs as well as the wrongs done against you, remember to go to the Lord again and again. His love covers a multitude of sins (1 Pet 4:8).

For Reflection and Action

☐ What temptations discussed here can you relate to? Are there temptations you face as a multiracial person that *weren't* mentioned? What are they?

☐ How are these struggles negatively affecting your relationship with God, others and yourself?

☐ Spend some time bringing these struggles to God and asking for his forgiveness and help in dealing with them. It might help to write out your thoughts and prayers about struggling with bitterness, self-justification, arrogance, opportunism, shame or other temptations. How will you turn from these things and think or live differently?

☐ Open up your struggles to a trusted friend who can listen and pray with you.

☐ How do you experience God's passionate and everlasting love? Are there certain activities or settings through which you experience God's love best? Make sure to incorporate these activities and settings into your weekly schedule.

6

All in the Family

It's 5:37 p.m. The phone rings and my mom answers. I can tell it's my dad on the other end because Mom begins talking about tonight's dinner plans. Mom's got her hand on her hip and is huffing about how it would have been nice to know earlier and she doesn't have anything to feed guests. I figure Dad is saying something like, "It doesn't have to be fancy, Linda. Just whip something together. We'll be there in twenty minutes." I can imagine it because I've heard it so many times before.

I didn't know it as a kid, but this common scene in my family home was a lesson in cultural differences. My parents, just by being who they are, taught me how to be both African American, a culture that expects the unexpected, and European American, a culture that expects the expected.[1]

My dad, an African American, is adept at "going with the flow" and enjoys welcoming people, regardless of previous plans or limited

---

[1] I am grateful for J. Nathan Corbitt's book *The Sound of the Harvest* for helping me to understand, and for giving me words to describe, some of the differences between my two cultures.

resources. He is the epitome of spontaneity. Sleeping in the car in a rest area or hotel parking lot is my dad's idea of adequate road trip accommodations. He'll make things work with whatever he has. These are great strengths of African American culture and traits I see in myself to a degree, thanks to my dad.

To my mom, a European American, thoughtful preparation shows others that she cares and makes for a better presentation. It also prevents unnecessary surprises. At my wedding reception there were beautiful handmade paper holders for chocolates and miniature bottles of bubbles with personalized labels because my mom is a planner who values attention to detail. These are great strengths of European American culture and traits I see in myself to a degree (except for the planning thing), thanks to my mom.[2]

"The more we know and understand about our parents, the more we know about ourselves. Our identity *is* tied up with our heritage" (Mains, p. 16). Who our parents are has influenced who *we* are significantly. We are often not aware, however, of how our parents have shaped our identities. This chapter will discuss some of the family factors that form how we see ourselves.

Can We Talk?

How much our parents talked about race and ethnicity and supported our emerging ethnic identity (or didn't) makes a difference.

"The level of the family's ability to resolve interracial issues becomes the basis for a consolidated sense of self [in the biracial child]. . . . Descriptive research on ethnic and racial identity formation indicates that open communication about race and racism within the family plays a critical prophylactic role in helping children understand and defend themselves against everyday racism" (Root, *Racially Mixed People,* pp. 84-85).

Roy was born in India to parents from different ethnic groups. The tensions surrounding their marriage and Roy's identity as he grew up

---

[2]I'm not saying white people are never spontaneous and black people don't plan or care about details. I'm referring to general characteristics of the cultures as I've experienced them.

were extremely similar to tensions experienced by interracial couples and multiracial people in the United States. Roy's family lived in the state of Tamil Nadu among his father's people, the Tamilians. In school he was not seen as a Tamilian, though, because his mother was from the state of Kerala and his features favored his mother's people, the Malayalees. Even though he was both, he was treated as the other. He was scorned and ridiculed because of Tamilians' stereotypes regarding Malalayees. He was on guard at all times, never knowing when someone would pick the next fight.

When Roy told his dad what he was facing at school, his dad did not condemn the hostile attitudes and unfair attacks. Instead he rebuked Roy for his anger and told him that the Christian thing to do was to forgive.

The fact that his father showed no anger over the obviously unjust treatment of his son, by people of his own ethnic group, crushed Roy. "I was devastated by my dad's lack of identification with me in my situation," he said. His dad's response compounded Roy's already conflicted feelings about being biethnic. He was not helped to understand or defend himself against the racism he was experiencing.

Now when Roy's Indian and European American biracial son comes home pained over a classmate's remarks, Roy first validates his hurt and angry feelings. Then they talk about how his son might respond to the offender, including forgiving the person.

Unfortunately, many interracial families don't talk explicitly about ethnic identity or racial issues. In her research, psychologist Maria P. P. Root found that the number one thing that adult biracial siblings she interviewed would change about their lives if they could was to have their families talk more about race (Root, "Color Lines in the 21st Century").

Author James McBride recounts trying to talk with his Jewish mother and black father on separate occasions about whether he was black or white and what he should check on school forms. "Don't check nothing," his mother said. "Get a hundred on your school tests and they won't care what color you are."

"But they do care."

"I don't," she said, ending the conversation.

His father said even less. McBride writes, "The question plagued me for many years, even after my father's death, and I never did find out the answer because neither he nor my mother ever gave any. I was effectively on my own. I searched for years to find the truth, to find myself as a black white man" (O'Hearn, p. 195).

It is possible that interracial families are talking more in recent years. Asserting and celebrating one's ethnicity has become more popular. I have heard young parents say they want to help their biracial children to appreciate their full ethnic heritage.

It also helps that interracial families are less anomalous and have more collective awareness of what it takes to raise healthy multiracial children. There are more resources available, produced by parents who have blazed the trail. The current thinking in psychology is that biracial people who are raised with a biracial identity (versus choosing one or the other) will be emotionally healthier in the long run. And there is a growing pool of literature written by multiracial people about the multiracial experience.

These changes are signs of progress, but what about multiracial people who are already grown and would have liked more help? Though not a complete answer to your dilemma, it will serve you to consider your parents' background and how able they were to help you understand your ethnic identity. You will probably find that they did the best they could, given their unique circumstances.

I first heard the saga of my parents' courtship and marriage over iced tea at a café after my junior year of college. That summer day when I was twenty, my mom told me how my white grandparents had responded to my parents' relationship. They had freaked out, pulled my mom out of the college where she and my dad met, and told him never to come around again. And there were other familial snubs. Extended relatives on the white side (Christians) later turned away my parents and me, a small baby, when we showed up in town needing a place to stay.

My parents' engagement and nuptials had not been the blissful, extravagant affair that wedding magazines tout. Race was associated with division and pain, even at the hands of their own family. The news shocked me—I had had *no* idea—but enlightened me as well. No wonder my parents hadn't talked about race as we grew up. They wanted to move on from the past and create a harmonious present and future. Their lack of discussion was an attempt to protect their children from the hard things they had faced, to keep us safe in a racially menacing world.

I've also realized that my parents didn't have any resources for raising biracial children. They were among the first people in the United States to interracially marry after *Loving* v. *Virginia,* the 1967 Supreme Court decision that abolished remaining state laws prohibiting interracial marriage. I honor them because they remained married through difficult times, and because they're still growing and learning how to do it better.

The good thing about my parents' outlook was that they taught me to respect and value people of all races and cultures. Many of my parents' friends were other interracial couples. Their crowd consisted of educated, liberal people and athletic teams where whites and blacks worked toward the same goal. Because of these things, my view of the world was that blacks and whites got along pretty well. Well enough to marry. Well enough to play together. Well enough to show up at Grandma's for Christmas and have a grand time together under one roof.

I treasure these images of whites and blacks being together and loving one another for who they are as precious individuals. It is a positive (and I believe attainable) vision that I strive for in my everyday life and community, and I'm grateful to my family for giving it to me.

The negative result of my parents' lack of discussion, however, is that I was not equipped with needed tools to navigate the divisions that exist between races in the "real world." I was not made aware, for example, of the economic inequities that exist between blacks and whites because of deeply entrenched systemic racism, or the pressures that my dad faced every day as a black man in white America.

Racial issues and conflict go hand in hand—inevitably so, if issues are discussed and dealt with in crossracial situations. I tend to fear the conflict that comes from talking through tensions (interracial or other) because we didn't do that in my family. Talking about race would have helped me to define my position better as a person who is of two races. It would have helped me to figure out where I fit and prepared me to face issues and people head on, with much more inner security and confidence in my point of view.

Our lack of discussion also contributed to my lack of awareness of how black and white people are different in U.S. society. As I noted at the beginning of this chapter, my parents are quite different, in part because they come from two dissimilar cultures. Never talking about this made it difficult for me to connect who I am with my ethnic heritage. I knew I was black and white, but I didn't know what that meant in cultural terms. (Of course discussion is only half, or less, of this battle. I also needed exposure to a greater number and wider variety of black people.)

After reading portions of this book in its draft form, my mom and dad pointed out that as young parents they didn't have the language to talk about culture that they have now. They didn't consciously withhold cultural information from me; there were a lot of things they just didn't know or think about. Working in higher education, they are constantly exposed to race and diversity training and events that celebrate various cultures. Now that we are more aware and have the language, we talk about it.

As I have explored my identity, I have fostered discussion in my family by talking with my parents and brother about what I am learning. I tell them about racially difficult incidents (present and past). I let them read my writing. I share multiracial resources that I discover. And they reciprocate. I have initiated conversations with my dad about race—asking how he has experienced and been affected by racism, for example. I told my parents that I would have liked to talk more growing up, and they assured me that they would do some things differently if they could do it again.

My brother, now also an adult, has been a great source of understanding. My writing has opened doors for us to talk about our experiences growing up biracial, including the pain connected to identity issues. He once told me he felt like a burden to both whites and blacks. White friends always had to be on guard around him or apologize for their racist family members. Black friends became suspect for hanging with a light-to-white brother. I related to this sense of being a burden, though I had never connected it to race. We have had several meaningful and insightful conversations about what we have in common as two people who grew up in the same household.

If you have a sibling or siblings, don't overlook them as allies in understanding your family and yourself. They can empathize with you in a way that most others can't. Even if they come to make different choices about their identities than you do, only they and God know what it meant to grow up in your family.

Bad Blood

Another factor that affects us is our parents' views of their own and others' ethnic backgrounds. We need to deal with how we've internalized their negative perspectives.

At a conference for black students, a Guyanese woman of African and East Indian heritage told the group that her Indian mother repeatedly presses her to identify solely as Indian. This biracial woman has to resist her mother's attitude as she strives toward wholeness in her identity. By being at that conference and sharing her burden with the rest of us, she was working to define herself apart from her mother's desires—an important step we all need to take.[3]

Scott, a Puerto Rican-white man, asked his adoptive white mother how she would feel if her biological daughter married a Latino man. She told him she would not approve of such a relationship. Scott was appalled and hurt. A Latino was not good enough for her daughter, yet he was Latino. As long as his mom maintained her negative attitude, Scott's Puerto Rican identity would never be affirmed and was in danger of being mortally wounded. He could not be a whole person in his

---

[3]Defining ourselves "apart from" our parents' desires is different than "in opposition to" our parents' desires—though the outcome may look the same. This is an important distinction. I recommend that you take the former approach; you'll spare yourself much turmoil.

own home.

When I met Scott, though, he was working for Evangelicals for Social Action and ministering in a black church. He had found places where he felt accepted as a whole person and could live out his convictions about justice and racial reconciliation.

Perhaps you have a parent who struggles to value his or her own race. A First Nations biracial man I met in Canada told me that when he showed interest in connecting more fully with his native heritage, his father said to him, "Being an Indian hasn't done me a damn bit of good." In spite of his father's discouragement, he learned more about his First Nations culture and is now a leader among Indian people.

If you have a white parent who struggles with racial guilt, you may have gotten the message that there is nothing redeemable about European cultures. Those of us with this heritage do have a responsibility to be conscious of social advantages we have been given because of our country's history of European domination. We will also serve future generations if we can learn to affirm the positive traits of European cultures without idealizing them or degrading other cultures—something previous generations have failed to do.

Nancy Perkins, the mother of Johnathan who was mentioned in chapter three, has helped her children to appreciate the emphasis on family among their Mennonite relatives. Having a large family with very close ties is a positive value that her biracial children can appreciate about their white, as well as their black, side.

The Great-Grandma Gertrude Factor

Your extended family has also shaped you. It used to be extremely common for biracial offspring to have little to no contact with their extended family members. For example, until the later 1960s, most Jewish and Japanese American communities rejected their mixed members (Spickard, p. 366).

When Jacob Pallas decided to marry a Polish-Italian Catholic, his Jewish parents were extremely displeased. Dating a "goya" was tolerable, but marriage was out of the question. They had already worked on plans for him to marry a Jewish girl whose parents they knew well.

When Jacob and Kathy decided to go ahead with their marriage, they planned two weddings—one Jewish and one Catholic—to be held on separate days. The Jewish ceremony was first. Afterward, Jacob's Jewish father proclaimed, "You're married now!"

Kathy's Catholic dad retorted, "Oh no you're not. Kathy, I expect you home at ten."

Fortunately for Chris, Jacob's and Kathy's biracial son, his grandparents' hang-ups didn't extend to their grandchildren. Chris was raised with loving grandparents on both sides and an awareness of being both Jewish and Italian.

Having relationships with both my white and my black grandparents, as well as aunts, uncles and cousins, has been helpful. My extended family has shaped me, and how I *see* me. They have helped me to know myself. I can't pretend I'm not white, because I have a bunch of white relatives. And when I struggle with the question *Am I black enough?* my husband quickly reminds me that no white person he knows grew up with a gaggle of black relatives. A good point—one I can't argue with.

My uncles and aunts taught me that "black is beautiful." (As a kid, I loved to don my aunt's enormous Afro wig.) My white grandparents introduced me to the Norwegian Club and the ecstasies of yulekaka, lefse and Swedish pancakes. My black grandma took me to her African Methodist Episcopal Church. When I consider my relatives together, in all their multicolored glory, and when I embrace them all, even the deceased ones whose photographs hang on my wall, I embrace more of myself.

It has also helped me to learn about my extended family history. After marrying in 1941, my black grandparents moved into a white neighborhood in Spokane, Washington, where they planned to have and raise their children. A petition to force them out began circling, but as Grandma prayed to her God, one by one their enemies started dying or being struck with polio until the petition disappeared! My dad was thus raised in a white neighborhood where he learned how to get along with white people.

On the white side, it was fascinating to discover that my Swedish great-grandparents opposed my Scottish grandmother's marrying their son. My grandparents then raised my mom to accept all people, regardless of ethnicity, which led her to marry a black man. The influences that have shaped my family have in turn shaped me.

Wassup, Cuz?
When our parents are not raised with a strong awareness of their ethnicity, this limits their ability to pass on cultural values, traditions and languages.

For some, race and ethnicity aren't that important. Many assume that how they behave and what they believe is just the way they are—it's not particularly "ethnic." Most whites grow up never thinking of themselves as having a particular culture other than "American." European cultural ideals and values permeate this country's ways of doing things—but white folks often don't realize that. This is a reality of being

---

For Parents
It is important for your children to have a diverse group of friends, and particularly friends who can reinforce what it means to belong to their nonwhite ethnic group(s). They must have peers with whom they can develop a sense of ethnic community consciousness, learn a common "language" and experience acceptance. *Peer* involvement is critical for this. Exposure to family members and adults will most likely not be enough to instill in your children a sense of belonging to an ethnic group or confidence about their ethnic identity.

Celebrate traditional holidays, attend family and cultural events, and visit sites that are significant to your ethnic group. If you have to learn along with your child, that's OK. Chris Pallas is very grateful that his Jewish dad and Italian mom taught him how to celebrate Hanukkah and Passover. This more than anything gave him a solid foundation for identifying himself as ethnically Jewish. They also took him to Jewish family weddings and funerals, where he learned how his Jewish people celebrate and mourn. And they regularly visited New York, where Chris could experience kosher delis, the Lower East Side and Delancey Street, a historical center of New York's Jewish population. (Chris is also proud of his Italian heritage and makes all his spaghetti sauce from scratch. Pouring sauce out of a jar would violate who his family raised him to be.)

---

in the majority: when your culture is the norm you don't notice it or think about yourself in cultural terms.

Members of some ethnic minorities, who are usually more aware of how they diverge from the dominant culture, also downplay ethnic differences. Given the history of oppression of ethnic minorities in this country, conformity for the sake of success or acceptance makes sense.

But remember that your parents' level of awareness about these issues can and does change.

My parents intentionally moved our family to the most urban area of Washington state (Seattle) so that we could be around more racial diversity. A few years later, however, my dad got the opportunity for a better job and so we moved—to a university town in a completely rural area where, other than the campus population, everyone was white. I don't think my dad thought much about how this would affect me. After all, his parents had moved into an all-white neighborhood inten-

---

Your child will at times be the object of racism. This is when your love and acceptance are especially crucial. Marcia, whose mother is white, told a story on an Internet bulletin board where parents were discussing how to help their biracial children: "When I was four I was at a community sponsored Easter Egg hunt in the all-white community that I lived in. [My mom] was standing close enough to hear me, but not close enough to stop a white little boy from coming up and saying, 'People love me more than they love you.' I asked why. And he said, 'Because you're brown and I'm white and people love white people more than brown people.' My mother tells me that she was hurrying over to stop the hurt she was sure would follow when I replied back: 'Well . . . my mommy loves me.' She says she knew right then that I would be OK."

No matter how well you love them, your children will still struggle at times with not feeling accepted or with feeling different from monoracial children. Help your child understand that he or she is unique yet still a member of the group. Like I say, "I *am* black, but I'm not only black." As much as you want to protect your child from pain, avoiding openness about racial realities is not the answer. Talking helps children to process their feelings, hear the hopefully more objective (and probably wiser) perspectives of their parents and form their own opinions, strengthening their sense of self.

tionally so that their children could have the same educational opportunities as their white peers.

My junior year of college, my parents moved to a city where there was a larger black and Latino population. My brother was in high school, and my father wanted him to attend the one with more black and Latino students. The fact that my dad encouraged my brother away from the predominantly white school told me that his value for ethnic identification and his acknowledgment of racism had increased since I was in high school.

Divorce

One biracial friend of mine doesn't remember his parents ever being together. Sometimes his anger about their divorce surfaces. "I know how I *don't* want to have a family," he told me.

If your parents are divorced, *you have been negatively affected.* One of the reasons God hates divorce is the harm it does to children (Mal 2:15-16). Children often internalize the separation as a statement about their worth, or they become jaded about the possibility of loving, long-term relationships.

An Asian-white friend told me that as a child of divorce her assumption has been that in relationships eventually someone will walk out; the question is just who will do it first. "I have a fear of things not lasting—it's both a fear of people walking away from me and a fear that I would walk away from a spouse.

"Everything is confounded [with divorce]. My belief that my love isn't worth as much as others'—is that an Asian thing or a child of divorce thing?" she wonders, alluding to the fact that Chinese culture has tended to devalue women and what they have to offer. "It's one more layer that I need to tease apart as I think about who I am and how I relate to others. Issues of relating to others become even more complex when you come from more than one ethnic background *and* more than one home. You don't have one microcosmic world to live in, you have two."

When I asked her why being a child of divorce might cause her to devalue the quality of her love, she replied, "It's that fear that I won't be

able to commit. Is this hereditary? Did I get a bad 'commitment gene'?"
After seeing her parents and other relatives go through multiple
divorces, she finds it hard not to suspect that her love, once offered,
would be less than effectual.

In an interracial family, not only is the child's view of relationships
or self-worth affected, but ethnic identity may also be severely stunted,
because one piece of the child's ethnicity is now more distant, nonexistent or, even worse, disdained.

A black-white biracial woman told a discussion group I attended that
her white mom is constantly telling her to dye her hair blonde and wear
blue contacts because the way she acts suggests that she's "too black."
This mother appears to have a serious prejudice problem. But she also
tells her daughter that she's becoming "too much like her dad." Her disparaging comments probably have as much to do with her negative
feelings about her ex-husband as with how she feels about blacks in
general. The poor relationship between this biracial woman's parents is
making it very difficult for her to have a positive ethnic identity.

My Asian-white friend above didn't experience one parent's being
negative about the other. She even spent nearly equal time with her
parents after the divorce when she was six. Though the breakup
didn't have a direct impact on her ethnic identity, she says it may
have impeded her ethnic identity development because a lot of emotional energy went into coping with the divorce and its aftereffects. "I
had to put a lot of time and attention into being a child of divorce,
just growing up and trying to be a functional human being. It was a
diversion of attention that otherwise might have gone into ethnic
identity formation."

A black-Jewish friend told me that after her parents' divorce, her
Jewish dad started urging her, "Don't forget you're biracial." It wasn't
helpful at the time, because she was encountering a lot of racism and
identifying more with being black. She knew he was mainly speaking
out of his insecure fear that she would reject him after the split, but she
had her own pain to deal with. "My parents got divorced during a time
of intense spiritual growth and growing racial awareness, so all of a
sudden I'm a black Christian woman trying to figure out how I fit into

this [Jewish] family."

Her Jewish grandparents, aunts and uncles had always radiated love and acceptance toward her. "But now that my mom's not there, I feel kind of lost sometimes," she said. "I'm afraid to fully be myself. . . . I really want to belong with them, but somehow I feel like my place in the family is insecure, and so I tend to downplay the me that goes to a black Baptist church."

She said she doesn't have the same problem with her black extended family. It helps that her mom's sister and brother are interracially married, but she thinks the difference could be as simple as physical appearance. "Even though my features are more my dad's, when I am with my mom or her side of the family, I know we look like we belong together."

When her dad started dating a white woman, it was very difficult for her. She felt invisible when she spent time with them, aware that people looking at them together would have no idea how she was related. When her parents were together, her dad had been the invisible one. "Before, he belonged to us . . . but now I'm the odd one out." It's hard to be enthusiastic about joining a white family, she said.

Finally, and perhaps most devastatingly, my friend is aware that the divorce has threatened her sense of wholeness. "It's like my parents' breaking up means that all those people who oppose interracial relationships are right. It's like there's something fundamentally unsustainable about who I am. I guess that's how a lot of children of divorce feel, but those voices get amplified when all the race-mixing stuff gets added to it. I know my wholeness comes from God, but I'm not getting a lot of help from society in a way that most people do. That's a good thing in a way because it pushes me to lean only on God. But it can be hard."

Dealing with Disappointment

If you are disappointed by the lack of discussion your family had about race and culture and wish your parents had helped you more in understanding and developing your ethnic identity, what can you do? What if your parents have communicated negative messages about their own or other races—even yours? Or if your extended family has rejected your parents or you? What if your parents are divorced? How can you deal? How will you heal?

First, recognize that there may be limits on what you can do at this point. You may lack access to family members due to death, divorce or adoption. Even if people are still around and are able to discuss these issues, they may not be willing. You can only do what you can do. You can't control how your family responds. There's also the unavoidable fact that you and your family can't go back and do it over. You can only start from where you are and move ahead.

Second, it's important for you to express your disappointment or anger over the ways you've felt let down or been hurt. Some families are better at dealing with emotions than others. Even if yours is not good at it, it's important that you articulate your feelings somehow— first to God, then to the one who hurt you or fell short.

Take time to reflect on your family's situation and the various factors that played into how your parents raised you. If you consider their side of things, you'll be much more gracious when you talk to them. Think about the positive ways your family has influenced you and helped you to take pride in your ethnicity. Also, remember that you don't know everything about your parents' perspective and experiences. Plan on asking them questions and not just telling them your conclusions.

If your parent tends to be explosive, easily angered by the slightest hint of critique or displeasure, consider writing a letter. This way the recipient has time to mull over what you say and can respond more thoughtfully. Letters can also be useful for communicating your feelings to a dead or absent family member. Even though he or she will never read it, this outlet for your frustrations and hurts, like the flushing of an infected wound, will help you to heal.

Sometimes our families are just not ready to hear what we feel *must* be talked about immediately. In these situations it is good to talk to a close friend or two. If you follow God, allow him to lead the way in broaching the subject with your family when the time is right.

In most cases, though, your parents will want to hear what you have been thinking about and will be interested to know that you have been wrestling with racial and ethnic issues for yourself. I have found my parents always willing to listen when I wanted to talk to them about the past. They may not always "get it" the way I hoped they would, but they have always proved themselves on my side as I continue to figure myself out.

Getting over our hurts takes time. Grieving not having had more friends of your race as a kid because of where you lived, or not having learned your parents' language, or of absent parents or extended family, takes time.

God doesn't take your pain lightly. He is close to the brokenhearted (Ps 34:18). None of your family's mistakes (seeming or real) will hinder God from fulfilling his purpose for you (Ps 138:8).

Think about the Jewish political leader Joseph, whose story is found in Genesis 37—50. When he was only seventeen years old, his own brothers sold him into slavery. God worked through Joseph's brothers' wrongdoing, however, to take Joseph to Egypt, where he eventually became second-in-command to the pharaoh. Because God put him in this position Joseph was able to save Egypt and many people in surrounding countries, including his family, from dying of starvation during a famine. Joseph learned from experience that God can turn family mess into a chance to bless!

In spite of the fact that I know God works all things together for good, I have grieved my upbringing at times. I have struggled with feeling as if I don't really count as a black person because I'm only "half black" and I was raised in mostly white environments. I've told myself that working for a predominantly white organization is not as difficult for me as it would be for a more culturally black person, thereby discounting my black cultural ways and downplaying my lonely experience as a biracial person.

One day God pointed out to me that I *am* able to function in predominantly white settings because of my upbringing—*and he is using this for good*. Otherwise I might not have stuck with this predominantly white organization as long as I have. I wouldn't have given my gifts to help college students know Jesus. I might not have learned as much about God or had as many significant black mentors and peers. In the context of InterVarsity Christian Fellowship, and through the diverse friends I've made within it, I have grown in understanding my fuller ethnicity. That was a helpful, redemptive revelation.

God will take your upbringing and the family influences in your life—good, bad, hard and neutral—and cause them to work out for good for you and others. You only need to put your trust in his ability and willingness to do that.

Another issue crucial to our healing is being willing to forgive.[4] Like grieving losses, forgiving our families is hard and takes time, but it's a nonnegotiable as far as Jesus is concerned. The only way to be able to do it is to ask Jesus to enable you—and he will. God's command to forgive is for our good, because, for one thing, it prevents us from becoming controlled by the past. But it also reflects the truth that no one who has received God's extravagant forgiveness has a right to withhold forgiveness from a fellow human being.

Even if you don't feel hurt by your parents, you might feel the need for more information from them. By asking questions of my dad I learned that as a child he didn't think God loved blacks as much as whites because of how much better off whites were. He internalized the poor treatment and condition of blacks as condemnation from God. My dad's reminiscences gave me further insight into why we hadn't talked more about race (or God, for that matter).

Our parents are a huge gift that God has given us in this life. Yet our parents can't be everything to and for us. We need to have realistic expectations of them. I have many black peers and mentors. These friends have taught me things about being black, belonging to the black community and knowing myself as a black woman that my father alone couldn't have.

God knew what he was doing when he gave you the family and background that he did, and he likes it that you are multiracial and multicultural. In the end, you can like yourself because your heavenly parent likes you.

---

[4]See how Joseph did it in Gen 50:15-21.

For Reflection and Action

Our identity is integrally tied up with our family relationships. Consider the following as you seek to understand and care for your family:

☐ Initiate a conversation with your parents or sibling(s) about some facet of your experience as a multiracial person.

☐ Do your parents have any negative racial views? How have these affected you?

☐ Hopefully you've had opportunities to know relatives on both sides of your family. If you haven't, consider how this lack of exposure has negatively affected your view of yourself and your ethnicity.

☐ As much as you can, learn about your immediate and extended family history. How have your relatives' stories shaped yours?

☐ Realize that one or both of your parents may never have been helped to understand *their* ethnicity, making it difficult for them to help you understand yours. They may have cut themselves off from their ethnic background. Your desire to develop your ethnic identity might be just what your parent or parents need to discover or regain their own.

☐ Has your parents' divorce caused you to feel awkward with one or the other side of the family? Is it threatening your self-worth, view of relationships or wholeness in any way? Who might you confide in as you deal with the pain of divorce?

☐ Don't forget to seek God as your eternal, perfect parent. Pray that God would show you his love for and acceptance of you daily. I often say a prayer that goes something like this: "Lord, please help me to know who I am, accept myself as I am, and walk in who I am today."

Solitude

Is it in you? Is it you?

*What is race? Am I black enough, Am I white
enough
I am me, is that enough
Don't speak I don't want to know
Labels need not apply; please do not apply
There are no vacancies*

Is it in you? Are you it?

*The error is unbearable, lungs rejecting/gasping
Placating, the solace that provides my strongest breath
I see more with eyes closed
This life essential sixth sense
Blindly, lovingly, I played on your side of the fence
The others wanted me
selfishly
Eyes closed—you deported me
And the pendulum swayed forever
Like the tide, drowning what was*

*I learn, listen, watch, expand, evolve
Involved . . . Excluded
I am too smart for my own good
Good?
Is it Lonely??[5]*

—IKT (ISAAC KINCAID TUCKER)

---

[5]Isaac Tucker was born and raised in Washington state, and he is my twenty-eight-year-old brother. He wrote me about his poem: "The words came from being biracial and growing up in communities that were predominantly white . . . with the small groups of black friends thrown in. Nothing in between. That feeling of never quite fitting in, but doing everything possible to do so. The last lines . . . signify these attempts at fitting in based on 'intuitive' perceptions of people, and how counterproductive that has been to my 'self.'"

7

As if Dating and Marriage Weren't Complicated Enough

I'll never forget the day my Shaun Cassidy Fan Club kit came in the mail. Opening that envelope surely would be the shining highlight of my prodigious eleven years. My hands trembled as I beheld Shaun's golden visage—a poster to hang on my wall. I had been transported to a heavenly realm and was gazing on . . . an angel.

For those of you who are too young to know, Shaun Cassidy was a teen idol in the 1970s who sang such great hits as "Da-Doo-Ron-Ron" and . . . well, that's all I can think of right now. But it sure was a great song—even if it *was* just a remake.

Shaun was my dream guy. He was white.

Of course I never thought about his race at the time. But looking back, I realize the culture at large and my immediate surroundings were molding me to measure beauty by a white standard. Shaun had become my yardstick.

The same year I became an official Shaun Cassidy groupie, my best friend and I regularly played *Love Boat* at my house. Our second-floor patio became the boat's romantic Lido deck. A white boy I had a crush on at school was always my imaginary love interest.

White boys were the norm at my elementary school, just as on *Love Boat* the television show. Except for bartender Isaac Washington and appearances by Scatman Crothers and Nipsey Russell, there were no black *Love Boat* options (and anyway, I couldn't pretend to be kissing someone who had the same name as my brother, Isaac, let alone a Scatman or Nipsey).

Even though I was being subtly influenced to visualize only white romantic partners, being in an interracial family sent a clear message that romance transcends race. When I found out that Patrick, an Asian American boy, had a crush on me, I let him chase me at recess just like Benji, the white boy who had a crush on me. When Mike punched me in the stomach, sending us both to the principal's office, I wasn't thinking about his race as we listened to the principal's cryptic explanation of spring and the frantic activity of birds and bees. I was thinking, *What the heck is this guy talking about?*

Only later did I realize that Mike liked me as "more than a friend" and that's why he punched me (ahhh . . . the logic of prepubescent crushes). Mike was probably Native American or Latino, given his features and skin color, but again, in my family race did not fetter romance.

But that was elementary school, where nothing is seriously at stake and race is not thought a barrier if it's a thought at all. With the onset of puberty and contemporary courting rituals come a whole host of new challenges. For biracial teens and adults, dating is another realm in which we find ourselves needing to choose.

The vast majority of our dating and mating options are either/or, while we are both/and. When I was growing up there was no Lenny Kravitz for a black-white biracial girl to swoon over. He was just getting over puberty while I was hankering for a hunka Shaun Cassidy.

Dating Angst
Many pursue dating and finding "the right one" as feverishly as if it were the cure for a fatal disease that takes its victims to the grave in a slow and torturous manner. At the same time, dating is perceived to be full of booby traps and pitfalls, sure tragedy and heartbreak.

For multiracial folks, the stakes feel even higher: How will people view me if I date a person of this race? How do I view *myself* that I would date a person of this race? Will my father/mother feel rejected if I don't date someone like him/her? Will my boy/girlfriend's family accept me?

Is there anyone out there I can date who's like me?

We want to know: Who will I end up with and, more important, what will it mean? And the questions only intensify when we contemplate marriage.

I didn't date much in high school. My options were limited to white . . . and white. The one date I had with a black guy was one that my dad set up. My sophomore year no one asked me to the Homecoming dance, and I was one of the princesses. I *had* to go to the dance, Dad insisted. So he recruited a local university student whom he trusted to do the job. I sashayed into the decorated cafeteria full of small-town, pimply white teens on the arm of Rico, a large black man sporting an Afro, and relished the bulging eyes and dropped jaws.

In college, I was overrun by an onslaught of black suitors. After a variety of nightmarish dates that I don't have space to recount here, I stayed with one black guy for a year and a half. Eventually I found that dating him raised various tensions. First, there was his family. I sensed his mother's disapproval, and though perhaps no one would have been good enough for her only son, I couldn't help but wonder if it had something to do with my complexion.

Then there were other black women. My boyfriend was well known on campus. Being on the football team gave him stature, visibility and popularity (and not just with the *black* women). He told me he was getting flack from the sisters because he was dating light-skinned me.

Dating began to be imbued with some angst. If I stayed with this black man, black women were going to hate me, or at least that's what it felt like. I had to face the fact that my skin color and physical features *had* drawn some black men to me. It was most likely a factor in my boyfriend's attraction.

The rumors I heard about black women's being upset about our relationship were hard to handle, and I abhorred feeling as if I was contributing to the continuation of the myth that lighter skin is more attractive. In the end I called off the relationship because we viewed our futures and following God quite differently. But the fact remains that dating angst is amplified when others make an issue of our race.

One biracial friend of mine with brown skin knew that as a teen she wasn't as attractive an option as her lighter, whiter friends. "I didn't grow up internalizing negative things [about being black]—except when it came to dating. That was too hard to ignore." When a new black boy was introduced into her diverse friendship circle in high school, her friends automatically tried to hook her up with him. Her senior prom date was a white friend, but his anxious, preemptive comments communicated that he was ashamed of her. "We're just friends," he repeated frequently to others at the dance. "Don't worry, I'm not dating her."

Someone a Chinese-white friend of mine dated on and off for two years separated himself from her because he didn't want to bring a white (or white and Chinese) woman home to his black family, particularly his mother. The breakup devastated my friend. "I thought, *I must be worthless.* . . . It was like he was saying, 'If only you were who you are in a different color you'd be all right.'" Seeing how crushed she was by this one incident, she realized how difficult it must be for darker-skinned people who experience romantic rejection regularly. She now realizes that the breakup has enabled her to better understand the pain of blacks and Latinos, but it still hurt.

Sometimes our own insecurities about race and identity create dating angst. Before the relationship mentioned above, my Chinese-white friend had been in a great, healthy relationship with a black-Latino biracial man. When a group of Asian American interns came to work for her employer in the deep South, though, she realized how much she missed being around other Asians. She abruptly ended the relationship with her boyfriend, in part because she suddenly wasn't sure that she could marry someone who wasn't also Chinese. She wanted her future children to be able to identify with that part of their heritage. Looking back on it, my friend says that even though her boyfriend wasn't Chinese, they related to each other deeply because they shared being biracial.

Who and whether we date or marry results from many factors, some under our control and many not: who we spent time with as we grew up, how we were raised, where we live now, who we know, our identities and personalities, how others perceive us, and the availability of people we consider to be options.

If you are strong in your ethnic identity, you probably don't see your choices of dates or a marriage partner as calling this identity into question. Unfortunately, most of us are not that confident.

"You're Dating *Who?*"

If we're honest, fear of others' reactions is often our number one problem when it comes to dating and marriage (besides finding viable options who are mutually interested—but that's true for everyone). We are afraid of rejection or that people will perceive us differently based on who we choose. We are not confident enough of our own identity.

Marrying a member of another ethnic minority (depending on their ethnicity) might get us flack from our extended or even immediate family. Our spouse's family, as well, might not approve of us because of our mixed heritage. An Asian-Latino man I know expects his future in-laws, whether Asian or Latino, to have a problem with the fact that he's not "pure." He has reason to prepare himself for this possibility: a Korean father refused to let him date his biracial Korean-white daughter, even though he let her date a Japanese boy.

In college Amanda Beckenstein dated a black man whose mother wanted to know, "How'd she get a name like that?" When she found out about Amanda's black-Jewish origin, she expressed disapproval of interracial relationships, then followed this up with "But it's not personal." Amanda thought, *How could it not be?*

Marrying a white, on the other hand, will put us even further outside the minority ethnic community or communities to which we belong—or at least so we fear. A Japanese American woman dating a white man writes of her turmoil, to which many of us can relate:

> Sometimes I flash back on all the ideas my parents taught me such as the idea that to marry a white man was to sort of degrade myself, and it's really hard to know how to deal with these kinds of feelings. . . . So I

look at him and all the feelings I have get mixed up and make me upset and dizzy: loving him, hating myself for loving a white man, hating him because he's white, hating white people in general, feeling underneath that I'm superior to white people, and even deeper underneath that I'm inferior to white people, especially men, feeling guilty for not having an Asian boyfriend, feeling that I'm taking unfair advantage of my social and sexual mobility racially when Asian men don't have that mobility, and being afraid of what other people think about my going with a white man—it's just really frightening. (Spickard, pp. 92-93)

The fact is, people *are* going to react and they *are* going to judge you based on who you date and marry. You cannot avoid this. The family of the great Israelite leader Moses spoke against him because he married a black African (Cushite) woman. God, however, seriously reprimanded the family (Num 12:1-10). God didn't like their bad-mouthing Moses, and he won't like it if others, on the basis of race, dislike a marriage choice you make in faith, either.

I've found that strangers more often assume that I'm white now that I have a white husband. But this doesn't make me any more white than before I married Matt. His race does not reflect the totality of my ethnic and cultural ties (or his own, for that matter).

It's a myth that marrying interracially automatically reflects one partner's complete cultural assimilation. It is possible for someone to fall in love with a person who is ethnically different but shares multiple values. In this sense they have cultural overlap (for example, practice the same religion, work in the same career field, come from similar socioeconomic backgrounds, have the same educational background and so on), but that doesn't mean they don't also have completely intact, individual ethnic identities. In a good marriage, people maintain and even deepen their ethnic identities and practices, influence each other positively with them and pass them on to their children.

For interracial marriages to work, there needs to be some amount of cultural assimilation both ways. For example, Matt and I have decided that we will seek out predominantly black churches to attend wherever we live because it's important for us to be involved in the black community and to have black friends. Matt has been willing to be a minority in these settings and to assimilate to black culture when he's at church. He's also contributed elements of his culture to the group. For example, in our last church Matt performed his folk-rock songs on acoustic guitar (though many had a justice motif, which our black friends especially appreciated), and he played electric guitar in the worship band.

Chances are that you have cultural overlap with the person you're considering marrying or have married. Otherwise you wouldn't have been drawn to each other in the first place. The thing you need to accept is that there's nothing wrong with this. Strive to be yourself, not the ethnic caricature you think others expect you to be. People may try to evaluate your entire value system based on your spouse's race, but if they do they're being shallow.

The need for strong ethnic minority families in the United States is often used as an apologetic against mixed marriages, or to argue that you as a multiracial person should marry another ethnic minority. This is an issue worth considering. But what if you belong to two ethnic minority groups? Which one do you choose? It's just not that simple when it comes to multiracial and multiethnic people. You need to marry based on your values, not someone else's. You're the only one who has to *live* with your decision, literally.

A family, no matter what its ethnic makeup, can be strongly aligned with ethnic minority concerns and values. Being committed to justice doesn't have a racial prerequisite. God's concern is with strong *families* (not just strong ethnic-minority families) who love one another and him, who do justice and love mercy. We should make these our highest priorities.

Most people who will make judgments about you are not close to you and have no way of knowing what your ethnic and cultural allegiances, identities and practices really are. If a person who doesn't know you has a problem with your choice of spouse, it is most likely *their* problem.

If a friend whose opinion you respect is concerned about your choice of spouse, talk with him or her about why. Maybe he or she will articulate a perspective that you didn't consider. Maybe this perspective will change your mind about marrying the person, but more likely it will enable you to enter into marriage more aware—of yourself, your spouse and how others will perceive you. It will enable you to address valid concerns and to reject invalid ones.

Maybe you will realize through your dating or marriage relationship that your ethnic identity isn't as strong as you'd like it to be. The good news is that you can work on changing that. If your partner truly loves you, he or she will want you to explore the fullness of your ethnic identity.

What Really Matters

What's of utmost importance is that the person you're dating or considering marrying helps you move closer to God and closer to who God means for you to be—ethnically and otherwise. That's it! That's what truly matters. Not what anyone else or their mother—or even *your* mother—thinks about your ethnic identity.

Does the person help you move closer to God? It's crucial that your spouse be a person who shares your faith and values. Having significant overlap in how you *apply* your faith in day-to-day living is also important. Greater tensions are likely to arise from not sharing religious convictions than from not having the same ethnic background. "Americans see race as a greater barrier between people than religion, when, in terms of cultural conflict between individuals, just the opposite is true," wrote Paul R. Spickard in a summary of his in-depth comparative research on interracial, including Jew-Gentile, marriages (p. 358).

After you're sure this person helps you move toward God, here are some questions that will hopefully help you discern if you're ready for marriage and if you've found "the right one." (By the way, I tend to believe that though God is sovereign and directs our paths, there isn't necessarily one perfect person out there whom you will meet and marry if you just play your cards right. Yes, good marriages require that "spark" that we think could only happen with one person. But they require even more hard work to love another imperfect human being—and there are many of those from whom to choose.)

First, have you established yourself as your own person? Do you know who you are and what's important to you? Do you believe that you are a valuable and whole person without a spouse?

You don't have to have everything figured out about yourself before you get married, but the more you know the better off your marriage will be. Likewise, you don't have to have your ethnic identity completely figured out. Most likely your marriage will be an instrument that God uses to further that process. But if you're not your own person, or you're using the relationship to meet a need for self-worth, you will put a burden on your spouse that is impossible for him or her to carry. You need to be confident about what you are bringing into the partnership, and be able to give to your partner as much as you receive.

Second, consider how race and ethnicity are playing into your decision. Do you think white features and skin are more attractive? Why? It might just be your preference (we all have preferences), or it might be racist conditioning. It would be good for you to find out. Are you marrying someone because his or her ethnicity makes you feel better about yourself, or because you think it makes up for how you fall short ethnically? Do some serious soul-searching and become self-aware. Seek to marry the right person, not the right race.

Third, what do you value in a spouse, and does this person possess those traits? I met a black-white woman who immediately wanted to talk to me when she found out I was married to a white man. She had dated many black guys but was now in a relationship with a white person, and it was getting serious. They were talking marriage. She wanted to know how I had known my husband was the right choice. It was clear from listening to her that she wanted to marry someone who was comfortable in a black world, had black friends and valued things black people value. I asked her if this was true of her boyfriend. She responded affirmatively, saying that he did inner-city ministry with black children and that all her black friends loved him. I told her I couldn't say if he was the right one or not, but the fact that he possessed traits that she valued was very important. Today, they are happily married.

How interested in your ethnic background and identity is your potential partner? How able is he or she to interact with your friends, whatever their races? Does he or she speak both of your languages, if you speak more than one? If it's important to you that your spouse be able to speak Spanish or Mandarin for the sake of communicating with your family or helping teach your children when they come along, you should be aware of this and make it clear to him or her.

How aware is he or she of racism? Or of other issues that are important to you? Is he willing to learn? If your potential spouse is not particularly interested in or aware of racial issues and is not very open to learning, that is a greater problem than if your potential in-laws are not very accepting. Consider your spouse's openness first—you have to live with him, not his family. Your in-laws can exert external pressure, but if your spouse is on your side 100 percent then you can deal with the pressure together. Plus, in-laws can change; your presence might be the needed catalyst. Your boyfriend or girlfriend *may* change, but changing him or her is not your responsibility. We don't marry people to change them, but to grow together with them.

Fourth, what is God potentially doing in bringing you together? Or put another way, how would the marriage be good for you? For your partner? I remember how amazing it was to realize that God loved Matt and me so much that he gave us to each other. We were good for each other, and God knew that. That's a major reason he wanted us to get married! Isn't God awesome?

God is so awesome that he makes our marriages not only good for us but also good for others. Matt and I share musical gifts and interests. He has musical expertise, and I am a gifted worship leader. We have made a great worship leading team and have been able to bless many through our spiritual and musical leadership. Not only that, but since Matt has studied and can play various cultural forms of music, and since I am biracial and bicultural, we can lead worship in a way that welcomes and brings together people from diverse backgrounds.

God's will is evident not only in the "strategicness" of a pairing but in the amount of love you have in your heart for each other and how eager you are to make a lifelong, unbreakable commitment to be together. When I got to the point where I was saying, "I could, but I don't *want* to live the rest of my life without this person," I felt that I could say yes to Matt's proposal. So do you *love* this person—both in your feelings and in your willingness to serve him or her? And do you accept him or her fully *as he or she is*, including ethnicity, in the same way you want to be accepted fully *as you are?*

If you realize you're not sure, or if any of the above questions bring up reservations, it makes sense to slow down the relationship. Certainly don't intensify it. Talk to your boyfriend or girlfriend about the issues that concern you, and definitely talk it over with God. A good spouse will promote the growth of your full ethnic identity and help you embrace your whole self; he or she will encourage you to become all of who you were meant to be.

Matt

I will never forget how I felt when I was getting to know Matt. I had never been so absolutely comfortable with a man in my life. I knew we could be great friends, and this was saying a lot about him because I had a hard time trusting men. I could talk to Matt about any subject or tell him anything about myself without feeling self-conscious or scared of what he'd think.

I also quickly found out that he was sensitive to racial issues and cared about racial justice. He had worked in South Africa for a summer with a national black Christian organization while apartheid was still in place. He knew about Cornel West, a black professor, intellectual and writer, before I did, and he bought me one of his books. As a jazz drummer, he loved the music of legendary black musicians. And most of all, he wanted to know about my experience as a biracial person; he was interested in *all* of me.

As our friendship and finally dating relationship grew, I found Matt cared about my development as a person, and as a black-white person. He wanted to see me have more black friends and input. He wanted me to be confident about how God made me.

Matt was eager to find a black church for us to attend. He built relationships with the pastors and joined the church's band—the only white musician involved. He allowed his life to be shaped and influenced by black people. He knew he had a lot to learn from them, and he loved them, as they loved him.

He didn't do all of this for me; he did it because he believed it was what God wanted him to do. But he knew it was what God wanted him to do at least partially because he was considering marrying, and then did marry, a biracial black-white woman. He wanted to take seriously my ethnicity and culture.

Matt helped me move toward God and to embrace all of who God made me. But when it came time to decide about marriage, I realized I was afraid to marry a white man. I already struggled with feeling on the margins of the black community; this would only make it harder, I thought. And my children—they would have no chance of identifying with being black, since they would most likely look even whiter than I do. I read *Black, White, Other* by Lise Funderburg during this time and wondered as I read one biracial man's story if I should try to look him up just to make sure he wasn't looking for a wife. Maybe I was considering marrying the wrong person.

In the midst of talking marriage with Matt, I went to a national black student conference. There I was immersed in black culture and got so used to seeing black faces around me that it was shocking to see white ones after I left. During that conference I asked myself some tough questions. Black colleagues I respect asked me hard questions too. Did I really want to marry a person who, although he was able to hang in black settings, was not and never would be black? I came home shaken.

Before Matt and I even left the parking lot of the airport after I returned, we were in a heated discussion. I wanted to know how aware he was of his own racism. Did he realize that as a white person he was, by default, privileged and unaware of ways he had been conditioned to think less of blacks? Matt was crestfallen and terrified. I seemed to be changing my mind. I didn't know it, but while I was away he had bought the ring.

In actuality I wasn't changing my mind. I was subconsciously testing (admittedly in a not very helpful way). I wanted to be absolutely sure that I could live with my decision, because divorce was not and is not an option for me. I got through my shakiness, and I have never once regretted my decision to marry Matt, who is a beautiful individual, not a generic white man.

My fears about feeling more outside the black community have been proven unfounded. It helps that Matt is quite willing to accompany me into majority-black settings. But beyond that, he encourages me to get involved. Where I'm tempted to shy away out of fear I won't be accepted, Matt reminds me of who I am and tells me to go forward with confidence.

It's been interesting for me to realize that Matt has his own bicultural experience. He comes from an industrious working-class family in Kentucky—they have shaped who he is significantly. He also graduated from a fairly prestigious private liberal arts college (the first among his cousins and siblings to do so), and he relates to academic culture in a way that his family doesn't. Like me, he knows how it feels to be of two worlds.

Regarding my fears about my children, we'll just have to wait and see because we don't have any yet. But I know that I will be able to instill in them a sense of pride about being of African descent, regardless of how they identify, because I have gained confidence regarding my own ethnic identity and I know much more about black history

---

Listen Up, Spouses!

What monoracial spouses need to be able to do is listen, ask questions, learn, and encourage their husband or wife about who they really are—some of us have a hard time knowing or remembering. They need most of all to accept their multiracial spouse fully. Many of us struggle with not feeling accepted, as if we don't fully belong anywhere. We want to be able to belong within the new family we are creating.

Good spouses will not discount any part of their partner's ethnic makeup or put down their partner's efforts to develop a fuller ethnic identity. As much as they can or know how, they should encourage their partner to pursue their ethnic identity and should join them in the discovery process.

Multiracial people often need to stay—or become—connected to their ethnic communities. Spouses need to be willing to be in the minority, even be uncomfortable at times, and develop friendships with people of the multiracial partner's races. They might propose living in an ethnic minority or multiethnic community and make it a priority to attend certain cultural events for the sake

---

than when I was younger. Matt has learned with me along the way.

If you're concerned about the ramifications of your marriage choice on your children, that's good. You should consider what life might be like for your kids, given their racial makeup. The advantage we have as biracial parents is that we will be able to relate to our kids as mixed-race people. Even though their mixture will most likely be different from ours, we can still help them understand their experience by relating ours. "What about the children?" didn't stop our parents, and it shouldn't stop us. We *are* "the children," and even though it's sometimes hard to be multiracial, it's good to be alive.

Though my children technically will be "whiter" than I am, and will only have one black grandparent versus my two, that was not enough of a reason not to marry the man I loved. My children's experience will be different from mine, but that's true of all parents and children. My children may have a more difficult time relating to black culture, but they also may not, since I am going to be more intentional with them about racial issues than my parents were with me.

I've feared that my desire for darker skin or more African American

---

of their multiracial spouse and children.

Growing to love the multiracial person's interracial family and making efforts to relate to them on their terms is also important. For many multiracial people, the family of origin is the one place where they have felt belonging. We want our spouses to accept our families too.

What's most important is that a spouse is simply *there*. Before Matt and I started dating, I met one of his friends from South Africa. He was of mixed racial background—black, East Indian and white. He spoke of how his relationship with his single-race wife had been healing for him as a person who didn't fit neatly into a single-race category. His government labeled him "Colored," but that certainly hadn't helped him know or value his ethnic identity and heritage. Healing came simply from his wife's commitment. He was free to be fully himself with his wife, who accepted him as he was. When he was crying because of the pain of being a mixed-race person in South Africa, she would sit with him, hold him and just be with him. Through this, he said, God carried him through his pain and helped him to become whole.

features for *myself* might manifest itself in a prejudice against my children, who will most likely be lighter than I am. This is something that I give to God and ask for his help with. It's a problem that is rooted in the evil of this world and its proclivity toward drawing boundaries based on color and features. I pray God will continue to free me from my color obsession for the sake of my children.

Spouses have an important role to play in the lives of their multiracial partners. May God bless you, then, as you make this important decision. This time, may choosing make you very happy and bring lifelong joy.

For Reflection and Action

Choosing whom to date and eventually marry is a huge decision. Perhaps answering these questions will help you as you think about the future, or about a current relationship.

☐ Do others' opinions affect your choice of dates? How secure do you feel about your ethnic identity and your place within an ethnic community? Are your feelings affecting your choice of whom to date or marry?

☐ If you're in a dating relationship, take time to answer the questions raised in the section "What Really Matters." Talk to God about these things; then talk with your boyfriend or girlfriend about any concerns you think are important to address at this time. (If you are married, most of these questions are also relevant to marriage relationships and could help you to identify areas of growth for you and your spouse.)

☐ How has rejection from potential dates or their families hurt you or damaged your self-image? Take these hurts to God and ask him to make you whole. Be encouraged by the truth that God has said he will never leave or forsake you (Deut 31:6, 8; Heb 13:5). Also, God has made it clear that when people revile his children, they are actually mocking him. He takes our rejections personally and will defend us. (See 1 Sam 8:7 and 2 Kings 19:22 for examples.)

☐ Give God any fears or prejudices that might prevent you from being open to a particular spouse he wants to give you for your good and others'.

☐ Consider how your choice of marriage partner could affect your children's experience. What cultural values, ethnic practices and history do you hope to pass on to your child?

☐ Talk with your spouse about how he or she can support, encourage and partner with you as you seek wholeness. (This chapter's sidebar for spouses could be a good starting point.)

8

Made Multiracial for a Reason

In the first chapter of Matthew, a Jesus biography written primarily to Jews, we learn that Jesus' bloodline contained non-Jews. *Jesus was mixed!* Why would God choose to come to earth in a mixed-race body? Why would Matthew, a Jew writing primarily to Jews, not cover up Jesus' multiracial heritage? He didn't have to mention the four Gentile women in Jesus' genealogy.

Matthew confronts people clinging to ethnic purity with the fact of Jesus' mixed blood. "[Jesus] choreographed into his own earthly body all the most theologically sinful bloodlines in the Middle East" (Bakker, p. 125). Tamar and Rahab were Canaanite, Ruth was Moabite (Moab was the ancestral home of Sodom). It is thought that Bathsheba also was a Gentile, since her original husband was a Hittite. There's nothing like a little race mixing to challenge racial pride and separatism, and God knows we need that challenge! So he came as a mixed-race person.

Globally and historically, multiracial people are not new. Ethnic groups have been mixing for thousands of years—with each conquest, exile, peace treaty or migration. (See appendix two for specific examples.) In the United States, however, where mixing occurred it was usually covered up or disregarded for the sake of keeping racial distinctions clear.

The growing presence of a consciously multiracial population has much potential to highlight the evil of our society's racial caste system and the depravity of the human heart that created it—to challenge racial pride and separatism just as the multiracial Jesus challenged New Testament-era Jews.

As multiracial people, we can either join God in rejecting racial hierarchies or we can reinforce them. We possess the potential to bring together the groups to which we belong or simply to become another tribe among warring tribes. If we are willing, God will make us mediators and mirrors of his reconciling power. If we are not, we will further entrench a system that is tearing apart society at its core.

The burden is not ours alone. The whole community is responsible. Yet we have a role to play.

Race Mixing and Winemaking

It is not impossible that the United States could come to a disgraceful, shameful and violent end if our racial problem is not addressed. We are not above the ethnic conflicts in Yugoslavia, Ireland, Rwanda or South Africa. We are not immune from becoming known as the "former United States." In the spring of 1999 two Colorado high-schoolers killed twelve of their fellow students and one teacher before committing suicide. They were supposedly Hitler aficionados explicitly prejudiced against blacks, Latinos, Christians and others. Most of us know that ethnic conflict exists in the United States; some of us believe it is one of our biggest problems.

When Jesus turned water into wine at a wedding in vessels normally used only for religious purposes, he upset the institutional order of things and acted in a socially unacceptable manner. He also provided the miracle that saved the celebration. He kept the party going when it would have ended in disgrace and shame because the hosts had run short on refreshments.

I believe Jesus is addressing our country's racial dilemma—saving the party—by making wine out of water again: he is bringing races together in families where, if they are willing, they can accept and love one another. Race mixing, like Jesus' original winemaking, upsets the institutional order of things and is often seen as socially unacceptable. Through it, however, members of interracial families often come to alter their attitudes toward other ethnic groups. They even become change agents in others' lives.

As I mentioned in chapter six, when my white grandparents heard about the relationship between Mom and Dad, they weren't exactly eager to hear wedding bells ringing. It was the late 1960s, and in some states interracial marriages were still illegal. In all states they were socially criminal. My grandparents were products of their time.

They forbade Mom to see Dad and told her she needed to leave college (where she met my dad) and get a job. Because Mom's heart was with her boyfriend and not her future career, the job search went nowhere, and she convinced her parents to let her go back to school under the condition that she wouldn't return to the relationship.

Of course she called my dad as soon as she stepped on campus. Sometime later, I was conceived. My parents got married with only two friends by their sides. The black and white families to which they belonged had no idea that their lives had been irreversibly altered.

Eventually my mother told her parents about her marriage and pregnancy. My grandparents realized that if they wanted to keep their daughter and have any role in the life of their first grandchild, they would have to change. They wanted to meet their black in-laws. If I hadn't been conceived and my parents hadn't married, this white couple very likely would never have crossed the proverbial tracks. Now they had family members who lived on the other side.

I was there—a newborn—when my white and black grandparents first met. I wish I had a video of that historic encounter. What was said? How did they receive one another? The potential for rejection and conflict was so great. It was 1968. Martin Luther King Jr. had been shot only a few months earlier. Black youth rioted in urban centers around the country. I can only imagine what tension there must have been as each of my four grandparents prepared to spend an evening with the in-laws they hadn't expected and didn't want. I can only guess the awkwardness they must have felt when they first greeted one another. My black grandma told me that tears were shed that night, and that's all I currently know.

Over time my black and white extended-family members grew increasingly comfortable with one another. I would dare say they even came to love each other. My white grandparents were forever changed. As my dad says, as Christians "they actually began to walk their talk."

When I was a kid, my parents invited an African university student to live with our family. We visited my white grandparents and brought him with us. My grandparents intentionally seated our exchange student between their two white friends at dinner. They made it impossible for these friends to avoid interacting with a black man and (so I'm told) relished every moment of the evening.

In the 1980s my grandparents' church protested a cross-burning on the yard of an interracial family in the community. My grandparents supported the protest. They had clearly changed since the time they found out their daughter was dating a black man. They sought to help others change too.

The transformation I have witnessed in my grandparents is the work of God. Scripture declares that God alone makes it possible for hostile ethnic groups to be reconciled into one body, as happened in my family: "For he [Jesus] is our peace; in his flesh he has made both groups into one and has broken down the dividing wall, that is, the hostility between us . . . that he might create in himself one new humanity in place of the two, thus making peace, and might reconcile both groups to God in one body through the cross" (Eph 2:14-16).

Jesus ushered in a new reality that made Jews and Gentiles, historically separated and opposed, into one people—unified in their desperate need for God to save them from death. Access to that salvation was not through ethnic heritage, as Jews had believed, but by faith in the death and resurrection of Jesus.

God demolished the wall between Jews and Gentiles, and he continues to do the same between hostile racial groups in the United States. He is doing this not only through the creation of interracial families but through the births of biracial people. We are literal reflections of the two becoming one that the Bible talks about, even if we don't always feel at peace within ourselves.

Defying Lies That Perpetuate Hostility

Multiracial people have the power to defy and invalidate lies that have taken root in this world and that keep ethnic groups hostile to one another. This power is manifested in our creation, through our words and by how we choose to identify ourselves.

In our creation. "Near my home is an eighty-acre tract of as fine land as there is in California. On that tract lives a Japanese. With that Japanese lives a white woman. In that woman's arms is a baby. What is that baby? It isn't white. It isn't Japanese. It is a germ of the mightiest problem that ever faced this state; a problem that will make the black problem of the South look white." This was a 1913 statement by minister Ralph Newman (Spickard, p. 25).

Here is another pronouncement from the same era (1910), by E. H. Randle: "All mixed-races are inherently violent, incoherent, incapable of national government, revolutionary, and are on the down grade of civilization. . . . Miscegenation is a sin against God and a violation of the laws of nature" (Spickard, p. 284).

Not that long ago Christians as well as others believed and taught that the children of whites and nonwhites would be a degenerate horror. After all, how could the offspring of "different species" be fully functioning and healthy? Mixed-race children were given the title *mulatto,* a word to indicate their mulelike nature—half one thing, half the other, and supposedly sterile.[1] Former Mississippi senator Henry Hughes called mulattos "monsters."

We may be revolutionary, as Randle said, but we are not degenerate. In our beautiful and completely normal creation we defy the lie that certain races are less than human, because we the offspring are biolog-

---

[1]Mules are often sterile because of being crossbred. The fantasy that biracial people were automatically born sterile fed the lie that they could not possibly be whole human beings and fomented antimiscegenation fervor (except when it came to white men having their female slaves—an efficient and pleasurable way to increase their property holdings).

ically just like everyone else. Two people, each fully human, create a third fully human person.

I think one reason God created me was to symbolize the vital, valuable and beautiful things that result when black and white people work together and love one another. Metaphorically, multiracial people display the life that flows from racial reconciliation.

Through our words. Being multiracial allows many of us to move fluidly between racial groups. Sometimes we hear, see or experience things that we know would be hurtful to our relatives and friends of the other race—and that are most likely hurtful to us too. We can help others to face their prejudices, misperceptions and stereotypes as well as societal racism.

Once when I was planning an event with white coworkers, the idea of using the color brown to symbolize the fall of humanity in the book of Genesis came up. I told them that the association of brown with bad in our society is hurtful to people with brown skin, including myself. Black is also often identified with evil and negative things. Some Christian groups use black to denote sinfulness, for example—a symbol I have yet to find in the Bible. My white coworkers took my challenge to heart, apologized and dropped the idea. (Another negative color equation worth challenging: "yellow," used in reference to cowardice and Asians.)

Another time, when a white person asked if it would offend me if she said she didn't see me as biracial but as a human being, I said I would rather she become aware of racism than ignore the concept of race. I offered some examples of how racism presently affects black people's lives. And I pointed out that regardless of how she saw me, being biracial was a major part of my life. So if she wanted to know me as a human being, she needed to learn about my experience of being black and white.

On the flip side, I heard an African American colleague quote a prominent black leader as calling white people "rats." The reference had to do with why there is so much skin color diversity among blacks—because white "rats" have injected their blood. We were in a large circle of black friends when he said this, and everyone laughed.

Later I realized I had felt hurt by this generalization regarding whites. (Was my mom a rat?) Although I'm told rats are clean animals that make wonderful pets, I've never heard *rat* used as a positive descriptor. I called my friend and told him how I felt. He said the quote was referring to white masters who had forced black women into sex, not to interracially married people in general, but because I brought it up he was compelled to verify the quote. It turned out that the actual word that had been used of whites was *cat*—a popular slang term when the 1970 speech was given.

I'm glad that I brought it up with my friend and that he took me seriously. He knows that I'm committed to the black community and proud of my black heritage. He also knows that having a white parent has significantly affected how I hear and see things.

I hope that both white and black friends and acquaintances will be less likely to generalize about people of the other race because they know me.

By our choice of identity. Madison Grant, in his 1916 book *The Passing of the Great Race,* wrote:

> It must be borne in mind that the specializations which characterize the higher races are of relatively recent development, are highly unstable and when mixed with generalized or primitive characters tend to disappear. Whether we like to admit it or not, the result of the mixture of two races, in the long run, gives us a race reverting to the more ancient, generalized and lower type. The cross between a white man and an Indian is an Indian; the cross between a white man and a Negro is a Negro; the cross between a white man and a Hindu is a Hindu; and the cross between any of the three European races and a Jew is a Jew. (Myrdal, p. 115)

We have power to defy and invalidate lies that have been perpetuated about ethnic groups through our identity choices. Some biracial people choose to embrace whichever of their races is most despised and say they are fully that. This is one way to reject the claim that certain races contaminate others—by embracing the "pollutant" race as beautiful and as the totality of their identity.

The lie that some races are better than others can also be defied by maintaining a biracial identity. A tradition in the United States holds that you automatically belong to the "lower" of the races that make up your mix (see quote above). This rule—called hypodescent and at one time enforced by law—has calcified the racial caste system in our country because it implies that there is a racial hierarchy. Hypodescent is a result of the myth that whites are more highly evolved and their stock must therefore be kept pure.

By saying I am biracial I in no way mean to reject, or even downplay, my blackness. I'm not trying to distance myself from my black community so as to avoid the "stigma" of being black. Rather, I hope to communicate that white is not so holy and untouchable, and black so corrupting, that they can't coexist. I want to end the wholesale vilification of blackness and sanctification of whiteness.

When we claim all parts of ourselves, we are saying, "There's nothing to be ashamed of here! All races are equally beautiful." By being comfortable with all of who you are, you can relativize the races. You can be a walking reminder that there really is only one race, made creatively diverse to demonstrate the multifaceted nature of God.

He has created us *all* to be "a little lower than gods" and has crowned us *all* with glory and honor (see Ps 8:5). Whatever choices we make about our identity, we need to make sure we are reinforcing this truth.

Blessed Are the Peacemakers
In claiming to be multiracial, however, we must be wary of making our own mixed-race category simply for the sake of fighting for our own rights and interests. It's great for us to have options on forms other than "Other." And it is helpful to have our own magazines or social groups (I subscribe to and attend them). We should not let people walk on us and tell us who we are. We should stand up and be ourselves.

Yet we could become too self-focused to be real peacemakers. We must not become yet another faction, another shard of a shattered mirror. Why not embrace the honored position we've been given as those who have potential to act as glue for the pieces?

My yearning for reconciliation between hostile racial groups predates my entrance into this world. Black and white are written together on my DNA. Sometimes I feel it is an issue of survival for me that they get together (it's not true, but it can feel that way). How can I, permanently a mixture of both, exist in a world where blacks and whites are forever separated?

When I see reconciliation, in fact or in symbol, it moves me to the depths of my soul. A white mother loving her brown biracial children, a black woman and a white man kneeling together at communion, a white man embracing a black man—scenes like this give me hope for our collective future as well as my personal wholeness. They reflect the fact that black and white are not inherently antagonistic or repulsive to one another in God's reality. They can coexist, even dwell in harmony—if in this world, then also in *me*. And if in me, then maybe in this world.

At a predominantly black church my husband and I belonged to we always sang the doxology while holding hands. At the sound of "Praise Father, Son and Holy Ghost," we would lift our clasped hands over our heads—powerful, triumphant. We were unified and victorious. I never felt more so than when I was standing between a black person and a white person. As we raised our arms, I would look up at our joined hands and pray, "Let this be my life, Lord, let this be possible, that blacks and whites be connected to each other through me."

There is no doubt that I am most comfortable in ethnically diverse groups. When a group is all one or the other I feel like the odd person out. To be the only person of color in an all-white group or the only biracial person in an all-black group is difficult. These feelings fuel my desire to bring people together, and this is a good desire.

I once saw two dancers—a white woman in a black outfit, a black woman in a white outfit—perform reconciliation through choreography. From the profound statement of their costumes to each movement they made, they were saying that reconciliation between blacks and whites is possible. I wept uncontrollably over the thought, tears of hope but also of pain. Because for now the chasm gapes wide. For now unity is the exception and not the rule. Even though Jesus came to make us one, humans still have wills with which to choose to do good or evil, to seek unity or division, to right past wrongs or to remain blissfully ignorant.

I mourn the chasms greatly. One reality that gives me hope, however, is Jesus' existence. Just as lies about different ethnic groups keep us distant from each other, the lies we have internalized about God keep us distant from him. The chasm is so great it is unbridgeable, at least by human effort. If such hadn't been the case, Jesus wouldn't have needed to come to earth as a both/and person—fully human and fully God—to invalidate the lies we've believed about God and to bridge the chasm. He brought God and us together, and through him our hostility is turned to love.

Multiracial and multicultural people are like Jesus in that we are both/and people, too. I believe we are *one* (not the only) of God's solutions for the problem of hostility and distance between ethnic and racial groups. Because of hostility and distance the need for both/and people, like Jesus, like us, exists. As Jesus' presence reminded humans that there was a problem between them and God, we are walking reminders that there is a problem between races. We confront people with their prejudices; we arouse people's subconscious fears of intimacy between the races.

Many of us have experience and relationships within the various races to which we belong. How might we utilize this social and cultural capital to help people from normally distant groups relate to one another? Others of us easily move in and out of different racial and ethnic settings because of our multicultural upbringing. Instead of bopping from group to group—being multiculti superstars—how might we bring people together?

We can't change hearts—only Jesus can do that—but we can introduce people to each other and interpret differences where necessary. We can be peacemakers. When done out of a desire to be more like Jesus, being a peacemaker is a joyful and life-giving process. It requires sacrifice, but not of one's true self.

When I served as a campus minister in Pennsylvania, one of my priorities was to introduce students to the value of relationships across ethnic lines. I wanted them to see that we can learn a lot from those who are ethnically different than us. To this end, my husband and I held a weekend student conference at our predominantly black church.

As part of the program we took the all white and Asian student group to the Sunday morning church service.

Before we went, I prepped the students; I culturally sensitized them. For instance, I told them there would be a lot of "talking back" at the preacher. In many of the students' churches this activity would be considered inappropriate or disruptive, but in the black church it's rude *not* to respond out loud to the preacher. When you shout "Amen!" or "Preach!" it means you're paying attention; it's a way to encourage the pastor and affirm that he or she is speaking the truth.

I told them that during the offering everyone would go forward to give their money. There would be music playing and the choir would be singing. This was not some form of manipulation to get everyone to give something. In the black community, church is *not* a spectator sport. Everyone should participate even if they don't have money to give, because we're celebrating God's goodness to us.

We went, we stuck out like a sore (pale) thumb, but the students were received very warmly and had a great time. We even got a standing ovation when the congregation found out we had spent our Saturday afternoon cleaning apartments at the church-owned senior citizen home. It was a small step toward bridging blacks, whites and Asians, but it was something God had put me in a unique position to do. Who knows how God might have been at work to dispel those students' fears about relating to African Americans, or to give them a yearning to see racial reconciliation become a reality in the church?

On a more individual level, I asked Lori, a white senior, and Sherry, a black first-year student in Lori's Bible study, if they would pray weekly with me for racial reconciliation on the campus and between God's people especially. I had built individual friendships with these two women and wanted to see them develop deeper friendship with each other.

The weekly prayer times developed our relationships, but God did even more. Lori became much more aware of her blindness regarding race issues. She was raised in an all-white environment, and all her friends had been white. In college she had a more diverse friendship circle. However, the more we prayed, the more she realized she didn't know anything about how her friends' ethnic backgrounds informed their sense of self or affected their experience at this predominantly white university.

Lori became passionate about racial reconciliation. She participated in a summer internship program in which she learned about environmental injustices in mostly black urban areas in U.S. cities. When I heard from Lori after she graduated, she often talked about ways God continued to challenge her to be a reconciler and person of justice—whether through a book she was reading on the subject or a black friend she had made at church.

After a year out of school, Lori returned to her alma mater to do campus ministry. Sherry was still there and was leading a Bible study for ethnic-minority students. Lori supported Sherry by praying for her and her Bible study.

It excites me that at least partially through my passion for racial reconciliation and the ability God gave me to straddle the fence between black and white, Lori and Sherry became better friends and Lori gained a heart for justice and reconciliation.

Maybe you're not a natural "people person," but you want to be a peacemaker somehow. *Prayer* is a powerful weapon God has given us to partner with him in his work on earth. God showed me recently that he had given me a strong desire to pray for black-white relations. For you being a peacemaker might mean regularly interceding on behalf of racial reconciliation between the ethnic groups of which you are a part.

Another way we can be peacemakers is by helping other multiracial people know their value and be at peace with themselves. One biracial friend of mine doesn't know if she'll ever get married, but regardless she wants to adopt biracial children so that she can affirm their identity as they grow. She told me, "I want to raise biracial children because I think being biracial is so great—it's a gift. There is a richness in who I am, a complexity that I like. I want the children I raise to see it that way. Biracial people still get a lot of negative messages, so I want to give someone, instead of that, a positive message."

Michael Ramirez (whose story was told in chapters two and three) noticed a trend in his Christian fellowship: over half of the fifteen mixed-race Latinos in the group didn't want to be identified with Latino culture. After being healed of his own prejudice against his Latino heritage, Michael wanted to help other mixed-race Latinos embrace their whole selves. He sought to be a peacemaker.

Jesus promises a great gift to those who are peacemakers: They will be called sons and daughters of God (Mt 5:9) because God is the ultimate peacemaker. For those of us who already know we are God's children and are experiencing the benefits of that relationship, seeking opportunities to be peacemakers is a way to emulate our good Father. For those of us who want to know God as our Father, the invitation is always open: being a peacemaker is one way to grow closer to God.

On the Margins
Paradoxically, being in the middle often means being on the margins. This experience can increase our compassion for those who are marginalized for *any* reason.

The first South African I ever spoke with was a Christian man who, under apartheid, had been classified as "Colored." He was multiracial. As we talked about our identities he stunned me with these words: "When I go to a city where the majority of poor people are black, I am black. If I go to a place where the poor are white, I am white. We must identify first with the poor." His example reminded me of Jesus, who became poor that we might be rich (2 Cor 8:9), who became human that we might know God.

Jesus gives biracial folks another multiracial role model (besides himself) in his story of the "good Samaritan." Samaritans were descendants of Jews and Gentiles who had mixed and married after the Assyrian conquest of Israel's northern kingdom in the eighth century B.C. Educated, skilled and otherwise useful Jews were carried away. The rest were left behind along with Assyrians who stayed to establish themselves in the land. Over time these groups mixed and married.

Upon their return from exile, Jews scorned the progeny of these mixed marriages; they represented the oppressor and the contamination of the Jewish people. Jews began traveling around Samaria, instead of through it, whenever they went from Judah to Galilee. They didn't want their feet to touch even the dirt that Samaritans had touched, even though the two groups had some heritage in common.

"Good Samaritan" would be an oxymoron to any Jew—except Jesus, who is recorded in the Bible as walking *through* Samaria at least twice. As he was teaching, he had no problem telling a story with a Samaritan as the hero. In this story robbers beat a man and leave him almost at the point of death. A priest and a Levite, religious monoracial Jews, come by but cross the road to avoid the man in trouble. But a Samaritan approaches him, has deep compassion for him and goes out of his way to care for his multiple needs—generously using his own resources to save the man's life. This mixed-race man is the one whom Jesus says we should emulate.

Most likely Jesus' Jewish audience didn't like the fact that he told a story with a Samaritan as the hero. That's probably why Jesus told it, because he wanted them to face their prejudice. I also think Jesus was saying that those who have experienced pain can have more compassion for people who are suffering. Samaritans, because of their marginality, understood pain. They knew what it felt like to be beat up by those who didn't accept them because they were "half-breeds." The beatings may have been more emotional than physical, but Samaritans could relate to pain nonetheless.

Like my multiracial South African friend, like the good Samaritan, we are to identify with the marginal, those in need—be the need physical, emotional or spiritual—in order to help them. God has made us as we are so that we have the capacity to have compassion for these people.

Being multiracial and multicultural enables us not to hold too strongly to any one ethnic identity. This allows us to go and be with others whom some might consider to be from the "wrong group" or too different. We know what it feels like to be different.

God is making us whole so that we can help make others whole. When our experiences lead us to identify with and care for those in pain, we find that our lives take on greater meaning. We have each been made for a reason, and God will fulfill his purposes for us (Ps 138:8).

For Reflection and Action

☐ Reflect on the fact that your creation reflects the multifaceted nature of God and defies the evil lie that race mixing is inherently wrong and causes degeneration. Find a way to celebrate that you were created.

☐ How are you using your words and your choice of identity to combat racist assumptions?

☐ God can make us peacemakers between the various communities to which we belong. That's one of the many reasons he created us. Peacemaking will look different for each of us, but consider: because of who you are, you probably know people who are on different sides of racial, ethnic and cultural fences. Have you been overlooking opportunities God is giving you to be a peacemaker?

☐ How have you felt marginalized or "beat up" because you are multiracial? Maybe you've literally been beaten up. How could the pain that you've experienced help you to have compassion on someone else in pain? Who around you needs lifting up "from the side of the road"?

☐ Draw a picture or create a collage that depicts what you currently perceive to be your purpose in this world. You can add to the picture or create a new one as you gain more insight into your unique purpose.

9

Where Can We Find Wholeness?

You and I know we don't need to be healed of being multiracial or multicultural. Perhaps, however, the comments, questions or exclusion of others have wounded you. Perhaps family members, peers or teachers have hurt you. Most likely you have scars simply from living in a society that is racially and ethnically divided and divisive. Perhaps you are living with a huge split down your middle: you think of yourself as only partially this or that instead of as a whole human being.

All of us carry around negative mental messages that oppress us. They take on our own voice so that we'll think they're a part of us and stop fighting them. *You're so ugly. You have nothing good to offer; why should anyone listen to you?* For a multiracial person, these messages often take on a racial and ethnic cast: *If your skin were darker/lighter, you'd be more accepted or more attractive. Your eyes don't look normal. If you keep doing that you won't be considered one of them. You don't really belong; you're a fake.*

We need to learn not to turn on ourselves like this. Instead of splitting ourselves into critic and critiqued, or into multiple racial and ethnic selves that resent and fight against one another, we need to become whole.

Fortunately for us, God is in the business of making people whole.[1] God introduced himself to the Israelites this way: "I am the LORD who heals you [makes you whole]" (Ex 15:26). Later God promises his people, "I will restore health to you, and your wounds I will heal [make whole] . . . because they have called you an outcast" (Jer 30:17). Have you ever felt like an outcast? Has this left you wounded? God says he will heal those wounds.

Our wholeness is a primary reason God sent Jesus. From the beginning of his public ministry Jesus made it clear that he had come to heal broken hearts (Lk 4:18; Is 61:1). This same thing is said about God in the Old Testament: "He heals the brokenhearted, and binds up their wounds" (Ps 147:3). These promises mean a lot to me as a person who has been brokenhearted over the racial tensions within and around me, as well as the racial wrongs of our corporate past.

Jesus Can Relate

Jesus revealed God's power and healing nature to the world. His touch cured people not only physically but emotionally as well. He cared about body, mind and spirit; he cared about people's feelings and relationships with others. Since Jesus is the same "yesterday and today and forever" (Heb 13:8), we know that he is still able and willing to heal those of us who need to be made whole.

The really good news is that not only is Jesus a powerful healer, but he can relate. While on earth Jesus racked up a number of experiences that make him well qualified to identify with multiracial people.

What difference does it make if Jesus can relate to our experience and our pain? All the difference in the world, of course! Jesus said himself that he was God in the flesh ("Whoever has seen me has seen the Father," Jn 14:9). The fact that Jesus has suffered what we suffer in this life means that our Creator, the God of the universe, is not distant and

---

[1]Words used for healing, in both Hebrew and Greek (the languages of the original Old and New Testaments), connote being made whole and are all over the Bible. Wholeness—including in our racial and ethnic identity—is something God wants for us.

aloof, wondering why we can't just get our acts together. Rather, he is compassionate. To have compassion literally means "to suffer with," and our God *has* suffered with us, as a fellow human being. He knows how we feel as multiracial people because as a human he experienced the same feelings we have.

Of two worlds. Like those of us who are multiracial or bicultural, Jesus was of more than one world. He was from heaven but also lived on earth. He was with God in the beginning and he *is* God (Jn 1:1), but he became flesh and lived among us (Jn 1:14). He had to mature like any other human being: spiritually, mentally, physically and socially (Lk 2:52). Yet he also declared that he was a King whose kingdom was not from this world (Jn 18:36).

Jesus knows firsthand the privileges and difficulties of being born into a dual heritage. Throughout his childhood and adulthood he had to deal with his dual nature, much as we do.

Jesus' two "races" didn't exactly get along either. He taught his followers that there are two sides in this world: humans and God (Mk 8:33). That's why he had come as both: to be a bridge between the sides. Being fully God and fully human, Jesus could represent one to the other. Along the way, he experienced the tensions that accompany planting one's feet firmly in opposing camps—tensions many of us are familiar with, such as wanting desperately for our various sides to be reconciled or growing weary of the pain of being in the middle.

Jesus agonized over his both/and position prior to his death. He asked three times whether there were any other way that God could get the bridge job done besides his going to the cross as the middle man (Mk 14:35-42). Before it was all over people would desert him and God would seemingly abandon him. Perhaps you have felt forsaken by one or more groups to which you belong. Jesus knows how it feels.

Not recognized by his own. The Gospel according to John tells us that people did not know Jesus when they saw him. They did not recognize him as the One sent by God to reconcile the two sides. John says that Jesus came to his own people—the Jews—and even they did not accept him. If you have felt pain because your identity has not been recognized and validated by the world around you, Jesus knows how you feel. If you have felt rejected by people with whom you share racial and cultural heritage, Jesus has been there too.

Jesus initially received a hero's welcome in his hometown. People there marveled over his wisdom and teaching in the synagogue. But as soon as he intimated that Jews weren't the exclusive beneficiaries of God's blessing, that perhaps they weren't the elite race they thought they were, they wanted to kill him. They threw him out of the synagogue and even tried to throw him off a cliff. They rejected him because he wasn't toeing the party line about race matters (Lk 4:16-30). It's possible you could experience this with any of your racial groups. If you have already, you're not alone.

Hangin' with the enemy. Jesus was infamous for the company he kept. His own people grumbled against him: "He has gone to be the guest of the *enemy*" (Lk 19:7, paraphrase). The Jewish religious leaders muttered complaints: "Why does he eat with *those* people?" (Mk 2:16, paraphrase).

He had no problem staying overnight with Samaritans (Jn 4:40), a people group despised by Jews. He even defended the Samaritans when his power-hungry disciples wanted to rain down fire on them (Lk 9:54-55).

Perhaps you have been considered suspect because you relate to people whom others in one of your racial groups view as the "enemy." Jesus understands that pressure. Though others perceived his actions and relationships as treachery, he never forsook his own; he loved the Jewish people. He literally cried over Jerusalem because those within its gates did not recognize God when he was in their midst (Lk 19:41-44).

You can love all your people (based on ethnic ties) too. You can love both sides. Yet it's deeply painful when they don't love each other. Jesus understands this pain because ultimately *all* people were his people, yet they distrusted and judged one another on the basis of race just as humans do today.

Though his Jewish people often did not love their ethnic enemies, Jesus chose to be different. He modeled overcoming evil with good and welcoming those whom Jews considered threatening. He worked to be a bridge between Jews and Gentiles.

Isolated and misunderstood. One thing multiracial people share is that we are most often the only ones like us wherever we go. Our racial and ethnic makeup is usually different than that of everyone around us. Jesus knows even more about that: He never met anyone who shared *his* background.

Many of us feel most comfortable with our families because we share a "family culture" with them. It can be hard, however, when even our parents don't know what it feels like to be biracial. Jesus can relate to that too. The parents who raised him could never know what it was like to be both God and human. When Jesus stayed behind in the temple during the Passover feast, they didn't get why he said to them, "Did you not know that I must be in my Father's house?" (Lk 2:49). They didn't understand his unique identity as not only their human son but also the Son of God.

Jesus sometimes got frustrated in his both/and position. He had to deal with human beings who didn't comprehend his divine lessons even though he patiently taught them with earthly metaphors. "Do you still not perceive or understand?" he asked his disciples plaintively (Mk 8:17). People's unbelief in him and their narrow views of who God could and couldn't be angered Jesus. He understands when people's narrow racial views box us in and frustrate us.

Very few grasped who Jesus was when he walked among them; relatively few grasp who he is today. He experienced the isolation that you have felt because no one can grasp or relate to who you are and what it means to be you—to be a racial, ethnic and cultural mix.

Confusing but not confused. Jesus' identity was one of the hottest questions of his day. When Jesus asked his disciples, "Who do people say I am?" they gave him many answers. People had various opinions about Jesus' identity depending on what he looked like to them (see Mt 16:13-14).

In spite of the confusion and controversy surrounding his identity, Jesus knew who he was. He called himself "the Son of Man," a title that emphasized his humanity, but he also told Peter that he was right to call him "the Son of the living God," emphasizing his deity.

Jesus held on to his both/and identity all the way to the grave and back to his throne, because although he lived to serve people, people were never his master. Their opinions could not sway him from his God-given identity. Jesus can enable you to resist others' opinions about your identity too. He knows what it takes.

If you have felt more like a controversy than a person, Jesus can relate. You are a person, not an issue, and Jesus knows that. He can help you remain human in the midst of debates over multiracial identity issues because he loves you. Accepting God's love through Jesus is what keeps us human and ultimately makes us truly whole.

The Source of True Wholeness

Not only Jesus' life but also his death and resurrection were about healing people: "He himself bore our sins in his body on the cross, so that, free from sins, we might live for righteousness; by his wounds you have been healed [made whole]" (1 Pet 2:24). Some six hundred years before Jesus was born, this truth about his life and death had already been spoken by a prophet: "He was wounded for our transgressions, crushed for our iniquities; upon him was the punishment that made us whole, and by his bruises we are healed [made whole]" (Is 53:5).

The cross of Jesus is difficult to understand. As a symbol it is overused and sometimes abused. Understandably, many don't want to examine or understand its message. Some find it threatening or guilt-inducing. The essence of the cross, however, is love. It tells us that Jesus loved us so much that he took the punishment humans deserved onto himself.

We'd like to think evil is only "out there," but if we're honest, we know we are prone to self-centeredness and hurtful pride, and not to love. We don't love God or others to the degree that God made us to. We deserve God's punishment along with everyone else. But Jesus took the hit, showing us the potency of God's love for us. Jesus not only took our punishment but our pain, caused by our own and others' wrongdoing, onto himself on the cross.

After the resurrection, a wonderful exchange became possible: We give him our brokenness in return for ultimate wholeness. The healing he provides is comprehensive. It is about being in right relationship with God, others and ourselves. It is spiritual, emotional, physical.

The cross is the answer to the ethnic and racial divisions that we carry around inside of us, for when we encounter its true meaning we realize that no race or ethnic group is better than any others. Jesus died for *all*. He didn't do one thing for Jews and something else for another racial group and a third thing for yet another. There was no ethnic hierarchy attached to his actions. Rather, his sacrifice stated clearly that all people are of equal worth to God. One racial part of you is not more valuable than the other(s). Jesus died and rose to put you at peace with God *and* with yourself.

Further, the cross says that we are one people with one God and one solution for our separation from God. God humbles us to realize that all people are on the same side—there is only God and humans. Those are the sides. The cross declares that the dividing walls of hostility, which have put us simultaneously on opposite sides of the ethnic battlefield, no longer exist—and never really should have.

None can be finally whole without Jesus' intervention. For those who want to believe they can make it on their own, the cross is foolish, abhorrent, useless. But to those who have eyes to see and ears to hear, it makes perfect sense.

Timothy—A Biracial Biblical Hero

In the Bible there are many examples of bicultural people who use their double heritage to fulfill God's purposes as whole individuals. Jesus was one. Abraham, Joseph, Moses, Ruth, Esther, Ezra, Nehemiah and Daniel all operated biculturally. Paul was a Jew, steeped in Jewish ways, but he was also a Roman citizen who knew Greek culture inside and out.

Timothy is of particular interest for us because he is explicitly referred to as having a Jewish mother and a Greek father. Timothy was biracial! The meaning of the cross would have been great news to him because he had firsthand experience with the major dividing wall of hostility of his time. Timothy's example can encourage us in at least two ways: (1) he gives us a model of how we can live as whole people, using our ethnic inheritance to build bridges between groups and to build the kingdom of God, and (2) his prominence in the Bible reminds us that though we may feel marginal in this world, we are not marginal to God.

When we first hear of Timothy in Acts 16, he is being recruited by Paul to join him in his travels. Jesus had called Paul to teach both Gentiles and Jews about himself (Acts 9:15). One of Paul's primary teaching themes was that the divisions that kept these two groups separated and hostile were anathema in the kingdom of God.

Timothy was a perfect partner for Paul, one whom Paul came to call his "loyal child in the faith" (1 Tim 1:2). He had a sincere belief in God (2 Tim 1:5) and had been told by his elders that he would be a great leader (1 Tim 4:14). These things were undoubtedly crucial in Paul's selection of him. However, his racial and cultural background made him a strategic choice as well. Being Greek he could relate to Greeks, and being Jewish he could relate to Jews. Paul was committed to reaching both groups, and to bringing them together.

Timothy's mom had taught him the Hebrew Scriptures from when he was a baby (2 Tim 3:15); he knew all the Jewish teachings and customs. He had never been circumcised, however—perhaps a reflection of his Gentile father's influence in his life. Once Timothy agreed to travel with Paul, he was immediately circumcised. Paul planned on continuing his ministry to Jews and knew that if Timothy were circumcised, as all Jews were, he would be accepted as one of them.

On the other hand, when they traveled throughout the Greek regions of Macedonia and Achaia spreading Jesus' message for the first time (Acts 17:14-15; 18:5), Timothy's Greek background undoubtedly would gain them access with people who otherwise might not have been as open.

Timothy, as a biracial person who was both Jew and Greek, was able and willing to put on or take off his "cultural clothing" as needed. He did this to relate to the different groups he ministered to alongside Paul or even in Paul's stead.

Over the centuries scholars have debated whether Timothy was a Jew or a Gentile. The either-or dichotomy has been around for a long time! According to the *Dictionary of Paul and His Letters,* "the Rabbinic

Law on the status of children born to a Jewish mother and a Gentile father was probably established by early in the second century . . . and thus it is likely that in the previous century [when Timothy lived] there was ongoing discussion and uncertainty about the status of such cases. Paul agreed to circumcise Timothy because there was some doubt regarding his nationality."[2] The doubt and uncertainty people have about you are not new. Be encouraged that you're not alone in your struggle but are joined with biracial people through the ages.

Some say Timothy must have been considered Jewish; why else would Paul circumcise him in the wake of convincing the Jerusalem church that Gentiles must not be required to be circumcised (Acts 15)? Also, they argue, it seems intentional that Luke tells us in Acts that Timothy's *mother* was Jewish—later the criterion for determining legal Jewish identity.

Others argue, however, that Timothy was seen as a Greek Gentile. First, Paul circumcised him because, the Bible says, all the Jews knew his father was a Greek. Timothy was publicly associated with Greeks. Second, most interpreters from the second to the eighteenth centuries considered Timothy a Gentile. Third, there is no firm evidence that in Jewish circles at the time Timothy lived the son of a Jewish mother and Gentile father was considered Jewish.

Paul was a genius to recognize and capitalize on Timothy's ambiguous status. Timothy's multifaceted ethnic and cultural heritage made him an able bridge builder. Paul had no animosity toward circumcision as a cultural practice. Timothy could rightfully claim this cultural practice as his own, and he did, in order to work among the Jews more effectively.

Timothy's ethnicity was nebulous while he lived and for many centuries after. No one knew "what he was" or how to categorize him. But that didn't stop God from choosing him, because God knew the reason for which he had made Timothy. Timothy was a reconciler—of people to one another and to their Creator. As a both/and person, he was

---

[2]Thomas R. Schreiner, "Circumcision," in *Dictionary of Paul and His Letters,* ed. Gerald F. Hawthorne, Ralph P. Martin and Daniel G. Reid (Downers Grove, Ill.: InterVarsity Press, 1993), p. 139.

uniquely outfitted for his assignment. To try to make Timothy either Greek or Jew is to severely limit him and the God who made him.

Timothy can be a hero for modern-day biracial people. Surely he knew the tensions we feel today. Race mixing was no more accepted when he lived than it is now. And yet he lived a powerful life, the effects of which are still being felt worldwide. He did not neglect the gift that was in him, though he was tempted (1 Tim 4:14). He set an example for believers to follow in Paul's absence (1 Tim 4:12). He was Paul's most cherished student (Phil 2:19-22) who knew all about Paul's teaching, way of life, purpose, character and sufferings (2 Tim 3:10-11). He was named as cosender of six of Paul's letters in the New Testament. He was the one Paul wanted at his side as he neared death (2 Tim 4:9, 21). Because he was so trustworthy, he was given the task of passing on all of Paul's teachings (which were founded on Jesus' teachings) to the next generation of faithful followers (2 Tim 2:2). Apparently he followed through on what he was given to do, because we have the Bible, with all of Jesus' and Paul's teachings, in our hands today. *And he was biracial.*

Journeying Toward Wholeness: Dave's Story
David Gibbons (mentioned in chapter four) was born in 1962 on a military base in Seoul, Korea. His father was there to serve his country; his mother was there because it *was* her country. Dave's conscious memories begin where he was raised, in predominantly white and Hispanic Arizona.

Growing up, Dave felt ashamed of his Korean mom. She didn't speak, act or get jokes like everyone else. Sometimes he walked at a distance to avoid being identified with her, feeling horrible all the while because he knew she was his best friend. His love for his mom and his shame over being Asian ripped him apart.

At school kids taunted him. When a boy called him "Chink" on the basketball court, Dave smashed the heckler's face into the ground. When another called him "Chink" on a bus, Dave sat, silently soaking in the sting of public humiliation.

One time Dave asked his dad, "What am I?"

"You're American," his white dad said.

Dave tried all the harder to fit in with the "Americans"—the white kids.

"My dad didn't affirm the Korean culture angle," Dave said. In fact, no one talked about it in his family. With his mom "language wasn't as much about words, but sight and touch." There wasn't freedom to express deeper sentiments with words because of cultural differences and the language barrier between her and her children.

When Dave was fifteen his parents divorced. The shame of the breakup proved difficult for Dave's mom to handle. Dave watched as she physically deteriorated and drank more often, seeking to ease her pain. He listened to her sing mournful Korean songs, and he often had to carry her into the house when she collapsed on the doorstep.

Dave started viewing his mother differently—not as an embarrassment but as a Korean woman battered by life in a foreign land and culture. As the eldest son, he drove his mom to divorce court and sat on the back row. Seeing her in such a Western setting, he realized how strange the proceedings must be to her.

"After the divorce, I got worse," Dave said. "I went into a rage against God. I couldn't reconcile my pain with a loving God, and I went into binges of drinking and partying." Dave didn't know what to do with his parents' split, or with the split between who he looked like and who he wanted to be. He constantly asked why God had made him look so Asian.

Then in 1981, during Dave's sophomore year of college, his mom was killed in a hit-and-run accident. Ironically, her death began the healing process in Dave, the reconciling of his internal and external selves. "I saw my mom lifeless—I still have a vivid memory of it. I began to see things in a different light. I saw what was temporal and what was eternal. Suddenly my looks were not as important; my body was not as big a deal. A strong foundation of eternal values came through my mom's death."

As Dave reflected on his mother's life, he realized how drastically being an immigrant had affected her experience. The realization that she sacrificed nice clothes so that her children could have more overshadowed his previous embarrassment over the way she dressed. "A lot of what I do is influenced by realizing my mom was an outsider."

God started to bring resolution to Dave's relationship with his dad during his junior year of college. "I had been elected to a spiritual leadership position at my university. The Holy Spirit started working on me. I was convicted that here I was going to be this spiritual leader, but I didn't love my dad." Their relationship had been strained after the divorce.

Dave argued with God: "But I don't have any feelings for him. And what about *him?*"

God responded, "It doesn't matter—you need to do it. Love is about commitment."

Dave obeyed God and went to his dad. He apologized and asked forgiveness for being a bad son. His dad responded in kind. "As I committed to [my dad and his wife], the feelings would come. Over the years my love for him has grown."

Resolution came with his dad. But Dave still felt ambivalent about being Korean. The painful experiences hadn't stopped when he got to college. At his university there was a rule against interracial dating, and Dave was not allowed to date white women. His brother, who looked more Anglo, was. The rule reinforced Dave's belief that he was unattractive.

Dave was also set on working for a white megachurch. Since fourth grade he had attended white churches. "I didn't see myself influencing the ethnic crowd."

Then, while Dave was attending Dallas Theological Seminary, a Korean man stopped him and asked, "Are you Korean?" Dave said yes and the man invited him to his room. The man said to him, "You need to think about working with Koreans."

Dave recoiled at the thought. "What? No way! I don't want to be involved with the politics," he said. But he agreed to go with the man to visit a Korean church in Maryland. The visit proved monumental. Dave's vision was immediately altered. "I saw the people there as a sheep without a shepherd, especially the next generation."

Dave told God he would work for the Korean church in Maryland if they offered him a job—but only that Korean church and none other. Three months before his graduation, the church invited him to pastor their English-speaking congregation.

The assignment was trying at times, and Dave realizes now that he made many mistakes. His first Sunday there, a sixty-year-old man told him, "You need to learn Korean," and stormed out of the room. He found out that many older people in the church hadn't wanted him hired because he didn't speak Korean and was married to a white woman.

At first Dave responded to this rejection with biblical justifications. "I thought, *We're supposed to be a people for all nations, to be reconcilers.* I saw it as my role to be prophetic. But I came across too arrogant." He stayed for five years and learned some good lessons. "I understand the immigrant mentality better now. It's a preservation mentality—trying to save your culture because that's who you are. I thought they were being unbiblical, rather than seeing them as protecting their personhood."

While Dave was a pastor at this church, a pastor of a huge church in Korea invited him to come and visit. Dave stayed for two weeks. It was good for him to realize that the world is bigger than the West, especially having been raised in Arizona where, as Dave says, "we're still *Orientals.*" "It helped me appreciate Asian spirituality. There is a high value on sacrifice, a commitment to prayer and meditation, and spirituality is more integrated into everyday life."

At the same time Dave was growing to appreciate his Korean culture, he was becoming aware that he didn't totally fit in an all-Korean church. Rather than lamenting that he wasn't "Korean enough," Dave saw the opportunity to start something for people like him who "don't fit in either homeland." He had gone from all-white to all-Korean churches, and now he knew that neither one was for him. "Who I am is *diversity,*" Dave realized.

Around this time he went to southern California to speak. While looking out on the city from the rooftop of a Holiday Inn, he sensed that he should move there and start a church. Then he heard God audibly speak the words "Psalm Forty" twice—not a normal occurrence in his experience with God. Verse 3 of that psalm says, "He put a new song in my mouth," and this later inspired the name of the new church.

After receiving the blessing of first-generation Korean church leaders in America and Korea, Dave and his wife left Maryland with their three children, having sold almost everything, to plant a multiethnic church in Irvine, California. They named it New Song Community Church and started it in their apartment with eight people. From the beginning they wanted it to be a church for all nations.

Dave's insecurities about being and looking Asian were more thoroughly healed as he realized his status before God and through his relationship with his wife. "I saw myself as a son of God and that helped me see the whole world more clearly. . . . I'm God's favored son, not an orphan who has to look out for myself or be manipulative to get my needs met. I'm not a misfit."

His wife, he says, has been God's good grace. That an outwardly beautiful woman would find him attractive and marry him brought healing. But even more, "the way she looked at me, she saw me as a whole person. Her whole paradigm's not about looks but about the heart."

God has gone on to show Dave that his looks are a good thing. "Having Asian features has given me a passport face." He believes a new respect for Asians worldwide will enable him to receive people's trust quickly and give him access to places he might not otherwise have.

He also sees his biracial, bicultural makeup as a gift from God at this time in history. "For our generation, diversity and race are some of the biggest issues. If you can't be a diverse person you can't speak to this generation. . . . The Lord's preparing me to address and impact my generation. Biracial people have a platform we didn't have before. God wants to give us a voice."

Dave is embracing all of who God has made him, and he is letting his voice as a biracial, bicultural person be heard.

As you continue on *your* journey toward wholeness and learn to enjoy being many in one, remember that God loves you (he wouldn't have created you if he didn't), he can relate to you and he made you as you are for a reason. *You are not a mistake.* He has an amazing purpose for your life to which he will lead you, if you will follow.

For Reflection and Action

☐ How does knowing Jesus can relate to your experience as a multiracial person comfort or help you?

☐ Jesus has the power to heal (psychologically and emotionally as well as physically), *and* he can relate, so why not ask him to make you whole? Asking God for help is the primary way we will reconcile all our parts and become all of who we were meant to be, since our Creator knows the purpose for which we have been made. Even if you don't know what you think of Jesus, you can ask him to show up. What do you have to lose? And even if you are not a "religious" person, you can talk to God. He has provided us with an excellent book of prayers, the Bible, if we're not sure what to say. Try this simple prayer for starters: "Make me whole, O LORD, and I shall be made whole; save me, and I shall be saved" (see Jer 17:14).

☐ If it seems that your struggle will never cease and your pain will never go away, God has given you a prayer to pray as well: "Why is my pain unceasing, my wound incurable, refusing to be healed? Truly, you [God] are to me like a deceitful brook, like waters that fail" (Jer 15:18).[3]

☐ If you recognize that your lack of wholeness is due in part to your own doing, you can pray, "O LORD, be gracious to me; make me whole, for I have sinned against you" (see Ps 41:4).

☐ If you ask God for help and learn to walk in his ways, eventually you will be praying, "O LORD my God, I cried to you for help, and you have made me whole" (see Ps 30:2).

☐ In the process of becoming whole, thank God specifically for aspects of each of your races and cultures that you appreciate and that you like in yourself as well. What do you like about being *multiracial?* Write these thoughts down to have a record of them.

☐ How does Timothy's experience encourage you? Do you think God

---

[3]God can handle this kind of honesty and in fact is disappointed when we are *not* honest with him.

can and will use your life to touch the world?

☐ What elements of Dave's journey toward wholeness can you apply to yourself, regardless of your racial mixture? Why do you think God made you multiracial?

Epilogue

The performer appeared from stage left, sitting on the shoulders of another. The cloak draped around them made her look at least ten feet tall. Her regal African headdress added another foot. They moved as a single person. She was graceful, noble, her head steady and her chin high. The auditorium was taut with anticipation as the carrier sank to his knees and the dancer's feet touched the stage floor.

Suddenly the air was alive with the beating of strong drums and the pounding of her dancing. Her limbs reached and pulled, full of electricity. Her shining, dancing eyes revealed her triumphant heart. She moved with precision and abandon, passion and complete control. She had control over her body—every move, every jump, every twirl. She belonged to herself. And we couldn't get enough. We didn't want it to end.

Her rich chocolate skin glowed against the warm oranges and reds of her flowing costume and the stage lighting. She was a Yoruban queen, fully aware of her beauty and vitality. She leapt with the joy of life. Surely the conch shells would confirm how good things were and always would be. As she gazed at the shells and their oracle, a terrible vision beset her. A calamity was about to overtake her.

From the depths of her gut came a scream so agonizing, so terrifying, that every nerve in the room was on edge with fright. Every heart was pierced. Two men captured her in the folds of a long piece of fabric and then used the material as a screen behind which she transformed before our eyes. We watched her silhouette writhe and contort as she stripped off her royal robes. Somewhere amidst the confusion her headdress disappeared. Suddenly her braids flew in all directions like flames licking her face. Suddenly she was possessed.

The screen was removed, and we watched as an invisible master flung her up and down, back and forth, across the stage. Her dancing turned into resistance, as she strained and pushed against the terrible force that had overwhelmed her. Every tensed muscle, facial expression and pounding of fist on the floor cried out in agony.

What was happening suddenly hit me full force. The queen had become a slave. This was the calamity the shells had predicted. Again my heart was pierced, not as a viewer of a dance performance but as a woman with African roots. My people had endured the torture of the Middle Passage. My people had lived through slavery. Women who conceived sons and daughters who conceived sons and daughters who conceived *me* had been queens stripped of their dignity and made to live as beasts.

As I drove home from that performance, a feeling of wanting to be only African American swept over me. I apprehended why so many mixed-race people of African heritage in the United States choose to identify themselves as solely African American. That choice can say, "I understand what my people have gone through, and I stand by them 100 percent. I would not dare belittle their suffering by saying I am anything less or more than black."

I feel the draw to this choice. I affirm that choice. I respect the suffering of my ancestors and honor them for bravely facing down every evil, inhumane act of cruelty committed against them. I learn from them how to be a woman of character. At the same time, I can't live as if I didn't also owe my existence to European ancestors, including a European American parent and grandparents.

I once heard Dr. C. T. Vivian, a leader in the civil rights movement, say, "Insanity is the difference between who you are and who you *say* you are." He was referring to the United States—a country that has insanely insisted it is the "land of the free" while keeping a sizable number of its inhabitants in literal bondage or some other form of systemic oppression. Vivian's definition of insanity, however, also works for me as a biracial person. I can't say I'm only black or only white and not be contributing to my own demise. I must live the truth of who I am, regardless of societal costs, or face the more serious consequences of personal insanity.

Choosing a title for this book was a huge challenge. The publisher recommended an option that resonated with me immediately: *None of the Above*. As I asked other biracial and multiracial people about it, it became clear that it would work. There was an immediate identification with the sentiment behind the phrase, a sense that we don't experience being fully a part of any one racial group. The title reflected our constant cry: our existence is not recognized in this country!

Novelist Paule Marshall once said, "Once you see yourself truthfully depicted, you have a sense of your right to be in the world."[1] "None of the Above" felt truthful for once. *I'm not going to say I'm something other than what I am. Are you trying to drive me insane?*

But there was something not quite right. The title stuck in my throat, as much as I related to the angst it expressed. What was bothering me was the connotation that "I'm none of the races from which I have to choose. I'm something completely different than all the rest."

The dance of the African queen, ensnared by a saboteur much more vicious than any European trader (or African betrayer), has always haunted me, even before I saw it performed on stage. That queen tells me that, thankfully, I am not "none of the above." I am the fruit of the above. I incorporate more than one of the above. This is the truth. And so I suggested that we title the book *Check All That Apply,* because it more closely reflects my philosophy that it is not that multiracial people don't belong to any group; it is that we belong to more than one. My publisher enthusiastically agreed.

We can find belonging with our various peoples, maybe not with all of them, but with those who share the same desire for truthfulness, for sanity. We will belong with those who are secure enough in their identity to accept us with our identities. We need to get with others who share our *heart,* not our exact ethnic makeup.

My husband wrote a song for me because he wanted me to know what a beautiful thing it is that I am biracial and bicultural. May you also know your true beauty as someone who God created multiracial.

---

[1]Paule Marshall, in *Black, White, Other,* p. 9.

Why You're So Beautiful

I know you haven't figured it out
How could you be both/and?
Not two halves but a whole—mysterious but it's clear,
And so hard to understand.
Like a good long laugh after a fight,
You're a story and sign of what's truly right.

Do you know why you're so beautiful?
Have you seen the sky when both the day and night are overhead?
And in between the dark and light there's a color seldom shed.
And the calling's high.
Now do you know why?
Do you know why?

When I look around this world,
I see you everywhere:
In music, even food; in everything that's art;
In the hope that the strongest bear.
When tension is transformed through resolution,
That's when beauty's born—it's like a revolution.

Do you know why you're so beautiful?
Have you heard the cry that pleads for violent conflict to be dead
When two who are from different worlds seek unity instead?
And peace comes by.
Now do you know why?
Do you know why?

You're remarkable, you're delightful,
You're precious and you're true.
Your entire existence shows just how much we've been wrong.
It lives inside of you.

Glossary of Terms

Bicultural. Similar to multiethnic; however, unless used in reference to a biracial person, bicultural describes a monoracial person who relates to two ethnic groups or cultures because of immigration, adoption, how he or she was raised, or similar factors (see appendix one for definitions of race, ethnicity and culture).

Biracial. Describes a person whose parents are from different racial groups. This does not refer only to those who are "half-and-half" but to anyone whose parents contribute two races to the child (a person with a black-white mother and white father, for example).

Hapa. Derived from *hapa haole,* a Hawaiian term that referred to someone who was of mixed Hawaiian and foreign or white descent—literally translated "half foreigner." Many multiracial people with Asian ancestry have adopted the title hapa and wear it with great pride.

Intermarriage. Marriage between members of different racial or ethnic groups.

Miscegenation. From the Latin words *miscere,* meaning "to mix," and *genus,* meaning "race"—interracial sex or interracial marriage. In the United States the word has especially referred to black and white mixing and has been associated with scandal and sin. In this book it is used as a neutral, not a negative, word.

Monoracial. Describes someone whose parents are of the same race.

Mulatto. Probably introduced in the late sixteenth century by the Spanish, this word meaning "little mule" is usually applied to people of black and white ancestry. Though adopted by some biracial people, it is offensive to others in its suggestion that the mixed stock of two races are physically incomplete (sterile like most mules) because of "crossbreeding."

Multiethnic. Describes a multiracial person who is ethnically influenced by his or her various ethnic groups. A multiethnic person can relate and communicate in multiple ethnic contexts because he or she shares some of each group's cultural values, language, history, common experiences and the like.

Multiracial. Describes a person whose ancestry includes two or more races. It can be used interchangeably with biracial, but it is more inclusive. Technically the vast majority of people in the United States are multiracial, but for the purposes of this book the term refers to those for whom being multiracial has shaped their identity.

Outmarriage. Marrying outside of one's racial or ethnic group.

Transracially adopted. Describes someone who has been adopted by parents who don't share his or her race or ethnicity. Includes biracial children adopted by parents who might share some of their racial background but not all of it.

Appendix 1

Race, Ethnicity, Culture—What's the Difference?

Race, ethnicity and *culture* are not synonymous, though they often get used interchangeably. While I don't presume to understand these concepts in their entirety, I have come to some conclusions about each through my own reading, thinking and living in a society that is racially preoccupied and ethnically and culturally divided. The following discussion of these terms will cast light on how I use them in this book.

Race

Although our current concept of race has been presented as scientifically based, in fact it is not. There is no set of Asian, black or white genes that all Asians, blacks or whites share. Geneticists have found that there is often more diversity within the gene pools of people belonging to the same "race" than there is between people of completely different ones (Usry and Keener, p. 22).

Dr. J. Craig Venter, head of the Celera Genomics Corporation in Rockville, Maryland, and scientists at the National Institutes of Health announced in 2000 that they had drafted the entire sequence of the human genome. Their findings led them to declare that there is only one race—the human race. "We all evolved in the last 100,000 years from the same small number of tribes that migrated out of Africa and colonized the world," Venter said.

Venter and other researchers say that the traits we use to distinguish one race from another, like skin, eye color and nose width, are determined by a relatively few number of genes (in the range of .01 percent), and thus have been able to adapt rapidly in response to various environmental factors over the course of *Homo sapiens* history. Equatorial populations developed dark skin, presumably to protect against ultraviolet radiation, while northern peoples evolved light skin to better manufacture vitamin D from pale sunlight (Angier).

Skin color and other physical or biological markers often affect how the boundaries are drawn, but race is primarily socially, not scientifically, defined.

> Genetically speaking, about the only thing any racist can be sure of is that he is a human being. . . . All human races are hybrid—there is no way to make certain that he himself does not owe a genetic endowment to other populations. . . . All racial identity, scientifically speaking, is ambiguous. Wherever certainty is expressed on this subject, we can be confident that society has manufactured a lie in order to help one of its segments take advantage of another. (Harris, p. 55)

European ethnocentric pseudoscientists built the formidable foundation of the racial construct we live with today. Before Darwin, scientists believed that Adam and Eve were Caucasians (white, like them); Asians, Africans and Native Americans represented their degenerate descendants. After Darwin, the conclusion was reversed: monkeys had evolved into Africans, then Asians and finally the "most evolved race," white people (Root, *Racially Mixed People*, p. 22). The eleventh edition of the *Encyclopaedia Britannica* reveals how deeply this belief took root in modern society: "In . . . certain . . . characteristics . . . the Negro would appear to stand on a lower evolutionary plane than the white man" (O'Hearn, p. 117).

We might wonder how anyone could ever believe such ludicrous schemes, but the truth is we all still live under their influence and accept (even subconsciously) many of their precepts. The message that "white is right" and no other race will ever achieve as this race has achieved is pervasive in our society. Science holds great sway in our world, and its omniscience and infallibility have only recently begun to be questioned.

Swedish sociologist Gunnar Myrdal argued in the 1940s that Americans would be better off to use the word *caste* instead of *race*. Though *caste* has static connotations—and relationships between races are not static depending on one's social class, region and time period—it is a *social* concept to describe a *social* phenomenon. Race is a biological concept which "carries not only static but many much more erroneous connotations" (Myrdal, p. 54). One particularly pernicious connotation: since racial distinctions are rooted in the natural order of things, *God* must endorse them—of course always as *we* view, value and rank the differences.

Race started with (and is still mostly based on) physical attributes: white pseudoscientists classified into groups people who looked different from them based on features such as skin color, eye shape, hair consistency and head size. These classifications, however, were never neutral. Certain traits, such as cultural mores and perceived levels of aggression or intelligence, were linked with racial distinctions. More or less value was assigned to each group's traits (physical and otherwise) forming, in essence, a racial caste system. The problem with this classification system, of course, was that the ones doing the classifying had their own biases, shaped by their cultural values, as they drew their conclusions.

As America grew, its races mixed, blurring the physical markers that had once defined groups. Racial boundaries necessarily became social and legal in nature, especially in regard to blacks. This was the only way the caste system could be maintained.

Consider the following anecdotal support for understanding racial distinctions as primarily "socially constructed artifacts": A New Mexico Territory court declared in the 1860s that the residents of an area were not Indians partly because they were peaceable, industrious and virtuous (Root, *Racially Mixed People*, p. 118). In a more recent situation, three brothers who were Houma Indians with the same father and mother were given three different racial classifications. The oldest, born before 1950 in Louisiana, was classified as a Negro because the state did not recognize the Houma as Indians at that time (they were perceived as a mixture of black, Indian and white). The second brother was assigned to the Indian category. The third brother, born eighty miles away in a New Orleans hospital, was designated white on the basis of the family's French last name (Root, *Racially Mixed People*, p. 23).

Similarly, the definition of who is black has changed with the times and the one doing the defining. In the mid-1890s a man named Homer Plessy, one-eighth black, seven-eighths white, was arrested for riding on an all-white train car. He took his case (the now famous *Plessy* v. *Ferguson*) to court and lost. The phrase "separate but equal" was born. Plessy was ruled legally black because that was the law in Louisiana. There were other places at the time, however, in which Plessy would have been considered legally white, because states used different percentages to determine one's racial status.

Within the "white race" there's been more morphing than on all Saturday morning cartoons combined. Originally Anglos demonized Irish and Italians as if they were of a different species. Now they're all viewed as white. With time and distance from their countries and cultures of origin, the distinctions have become less important.

The Office of Management and Budget, which sets standards for collecting racial data in the United States (such as in the census), currently defines *white* as "a person having origins in any of the original peoples of Europe, the Middle East, or North Africa." I have a feeling that *white* hasn't always been defined as such, but for now it is.

In the 1940s it was deemed politically important to separate the Japanese from other Asians, for the sake of placing them in internment camps. Now, for the most part, Asian Americans are grouped together. A pan-Asian movement among Asian Americans was one factor that precipitated this shift.

Any standard that is determined by laws, politics, people's perceptions and shifting cultural values cannot be a scientific construct. Clearly, from the above examples, race has been determined by all of these.

This is an important distinction to make because beliefs "proved" or supported by science take deeper root in Western-influenced minds and societies. Historically, anything backed by science (as race was) quickly became "the way things were meant to be." From there it was an easy jump to "the way God set it up." And suddenly God was being invoked to keep the race construct (and racism) intact.

In fact, nowhere in the Bible does God command people to be divided among the five major racial categories currently used in the United States (American Indian/Alaska Native, Asian, black/African American, Native Hawaiian/Other Pacific Islander, white). Nor does God ever say anything about some people being more evolved than others.

Ethnicity

The concept of ethnicity *is* in the Bible. After the great flood, Noah's three sons and their wives repopulate the earth. In their multiplying and migrating, the nations (or *ethnos* in Greek) are formed, each with its own language (Gen 10).

Race *as we have learned it* is not supported in the Bible, but there is a sanctioning of different ethnic groups. Part of God's plan for our world seems to include the creation of distinctive people groups, each with its own language, values, practices, even physical attributes. However, a hierarchy among these groups—a deterioration from white to black or evolution from black to white, which again are racial, not ethnic, terms—is *never* indicated.

Of course the term *ethnicity* is no more sacred than the term *race*. Ethnocentric hierarchies are applied to ethnic groups the same way racist hierarchies are applied to races. The term *ethnicity*, however, is derived from the Greek word *ethnos*, which is used repeatedly in Scripture to refer to different nations or tribes. God has planted within each ethnic group an element of his wisdom and character, a portion of his "riches" (Is 60:5; Rev 21:24-26). This makes each group crucial in God's plan to reveal his glory to the world. It is clear that there will be representatives from every *ethnos*—nation, tribe and tongue— worshiping Jesus in heaven (Rev 7:9).

Some Christians use Scriptures such as Revelation 7 to argue that God wants ethnic distinctions to remain intact, and thus people should not intermarry and have mixed-ethnicity children. It would blur the distinctions. While it is true that according to the Bible ethnicity is not just for earth but also for heaven, what these Christians fail to realize is that I no less represent an ethnic group simply because I am mixed. I represent *multiple* ethnic groups. Furthermore, if they are going to insist that members of various *ethnos* (again, this is different from the concept of race) should not mix, then they best be certain that they have not married outside of their tribe of origin as well. Scots better not be married to Germans, or Italians to Swedes!

Though Christians have also tried to justify their anti-intermarriage beliefs with passages like Deuteronomy 7:3, 1 Kings 11:1-2 and Nehemiah 13:23-25, in context it is clear that God is not concerned about racial mixing but syncretism and idol worship. Marrying a person who doesn't worship God increases the chances that the believing spouse will drift from God, and the offspring won't be raised to know God.

Ethnicity, then, refers to the people group from which one descends. (African Americans have the challenge of not knowing our true ethnicity because of slavery. We've had to reestablish our ethnic identity in America.) It refers to a group's corporate history, sense of kinship, language, holidays and celebrations, customs, values and other characteristics, including physical traits, based on lineage. It is much more than what you look like (on which race was primarily founded). But it is inherited, like physical appearance, in that you are born to a certain *ethnos.*

Race is a human-made construct for carrying out human purposes. This construct is mostly inflexible and does not allow for mixture. It is based on external appearances. Races are not seen as being on a continuum but as separate, "pure" categories to which people are assigned. In reality there is no such thing as a pure race—especially in the United States—even though the survival of racist thinking depends on this myth. As soon as a white supremacist (or any white person for that matter) admits that he or she is not purely "white," he or she can no longer argue that white people are superior without putting himself or herself in the "inferior" category.

Race *can* intersect with ethnicity—but it doesn't always. A man with dark brown skin in the United States might automatically be categorized racially by others as "black" because of how he looks. Many assumptions would be made about his values, political allegiances and musical tastes. His ethnicity, however, might be Nigerian, Cuban, Surinamese or even East Indian.

Unlike race, which is a human construct, ethnicity is created by God to fulfill *his* purposes. "From one blood he made all nations *[ethnos]* to inhabit the whole earth, and he allotted the times of their existence and the boundaries of the places where they would live, so that they would search for God and perhaps grope for him and find him" (Acts 17:26-27).

Mixture is inherent in this understanding of how the earth was populated. For example, God brought forth Mexicans as Indians, Spaniards and Africans mixed together in the place we know as Mexico. Similarly, God birthed African Americans in the land we know as America, and we are a mixture of Africans, Europeans and Native Americans. Although the brutal treatment of indigenous Americans and Africans was not of God, I believe God envisioned and desired new ethnic groups and so created African Americans and various Latin American peoples in the lands where they now live. It would seem that ethnic groups continue to form, or perhaps transform, as people migrate, mix and develop new languages—and as God desires.

According to Acts 17, all human beings came from the same "blood"—a good response to any who think racial groups have disparate bloods. Furthermore, this Scripture says God made us to belong to ethnic groups in different parts of the world at different times not for the sake of separating ourselves from or oppressing one another, but that we might all find him. How God does this only God knows, but he does it.

"Although the U.S. has well-defined national boundaries, an ethnic American is an elusive concept" (Sung, p. 32). In the United States, because of the nation's size, diversity, and history of immigration and racial discrimination, ethnic identity is more often rooted in race or ancestral origin than in our shared heritage as Americans. While none of us, except perhaps First Nations people, can say that our ethnicity originates in America, all of us who call ourselves Americans share some cultural traits.

Culture

Culture is a vague term, hard to pin down. It comes from the Latin word *colere*, meaning "to till," and is related to the word *cultivate*. *Culture* originally referred to the improvement (or cultivation) of land and then later to the development or refinement of the mind, emotions, manners and tastes.

In our vernacular *culture* connotes "the ideas, customs, skills, arts, etc. of a given people in a given period" (*Webster's New World Dictionary,* p. 345). Thus Americans, though of many different ethnic groups, can in some ways be seen as belonging to one large culture. For example, we all live under the same Bill of Rights that defends our civil liberties, and all Americans value freedom and individual rights to some degree (though not all have had equal access to these). We all observe Presidents' Day, Memorial Day, Thanksgiving and Martin Luther King Jr. Day—even if it's just noticing their presence on a calendar and having a day off from work. American culture is composed of multiple subcultures, such as urban dwellers, small farm owners and extreme sports enthusiasts.

Culture and ethnicity intersect in that ethnic groups have certain cultural values and practices. However, *culture* is a much broader term and could refer to groups besides those descended from the same nation or people group (for example, "jock culture," "artist culture," "church culture"). Your culture, or subculture, is influenced by factors such as your family, where you live, your economic status, level of education, religious practices, interests, skills and ethnic background.

An interesting view of culture comes from anthropologist James Watson: "Culture is not something that people inherit as an undifferentiated bloc of knowledge from their ancestors. Culture is a set of ideas, reactions, and expectations that is constantly changing as people and groups themselves change" (Zwingle).

Appendix 2

We're Not Alone:
Historical Examples of Multiracial People

We've been made for a reason, but we're not the first multiracial people to come along. The history of racial mixing is world history. The Egyptians, for example, were born of African and Western Asiatic peoples migrating to that region and intermingling (circa 3000-5000 B.C.). Egypt's mixture eventually entered the veins of those descended from the Jewish patriarch Abraham. Many of Abraham's servants, given to him by the pharaoh, were Egyptians (Gen 12:16). It is quite likely during this period that the pharaoh would also have given Abraham servants from Nubia, a former northeast African kingdom of "Negroid people with some Caucasoid admixture" (*Webster's New World Dictionary*, p. 975). The offspring of these servants were passed down from Abraham to Isaac to Jacob and eventually would be defined as part of Israel during Israel's enslavement in Egypt—a situation that would encourage intermixing. Undoubtedly, then, individual Israelites by Moses' day had genetic roots in both northeast Africa and southwest Asia (Usry & Keener, p. 73).

Egyptians saw Hebrews as a different race; to eat with a Hebrew was considered an abomination (Gen 43:32). The two ethnic groups had a history of prejudice similar to any two races in America. Nevertheless, Joseph (a son of Jacob and one of the heads of the twelve tribes of Israel) married an Egyptian woman and bore two biracial sons, Ephraim and Manasseh (Gen 41:50), automatically making Israel nearly 10 percent Egyptian.[1]

Joshua, Moses' replacement and the man appointed by God to lead the Israelites into the Promised Land, descended from Ephraim and was therefore a mixed brother. And we know that Moses married a black African Cushite woman. They had descendants who would have entered the Promised Land with Joshua—a land flowing with milk, honey and mixed blood.

The New World

The history of North and South America is full of miscegenation—starting from the moment Europeans and Africans joined American Indians on these continents. As early as the 1570s, Spanish explorers in the New World used the term *mulatto,* indicating people of mixed American Indian and African ancestry.[2] The earliest English definition of *mulatto* (dated sometime between 1617 and 1623) states that a mulatto is "the child of a 'blackamoor' (African) and one of another nation" (Forbes, p. 21). Most likely the English used *mulatto* for a wide range of brown mixed-race people whose precise ancestry would never be known. For example, a 1656 definition of mulatto said simply "one that is of a mongrel complexion" (*Journal of Ethnic Studies,* p. 23). Though less than complimentary, this definition and others prove that there were multiracial people being born in America from its very foundations.

In spite of the clear presence of multiracial people throughout the history of the United States, we have been continually overlooked—treated as invisible because our existence makes interracial sexual relations visible. Perhaps even more threatening, we have proved since the beginning that there is no fundamental genetic difference between people. We are unavoidable evidence for human equality, something the "founding fathers" wrote about but didn't apply to all.

Brewton Berry, who studied long-established, isolated communities of mixed-race people ("mestizos") in the United States, noted in 1963 "the white man's contacts with the mestizos are brief, rare, and superficial. The mestizo is seldom the topic of conversation. He is never the subject of talks at Rotary, Kiwanis, book clubs, or missionary societies. He is rarely mentioned in the newspapers, and schoolbooks omit all reference to him" (Berry, p. 54). Histori-

---

[1]The descendants of these two biracial men were considered full members in the nation of Israel and received an inheritance of land along with the rest of the Israelites when they entered Canaan. (See Numbers 26:28, 53.)

[2]Africans first came to North America with the Spanish as explorers, not as slaves.

cally, multiracial people have been a taboo subject. But we have always been here.

Initially in this country, the mixture involved various combinations of blacks, American Indians and whites. Asian mixed-race people didn't begin to appear until the late nineteenth and early twentieth centuries, when Chinese first migrated to the United States, followed by Japanese, Filipinos and Koreans.

By definition, most people called Latinos, Hispanics or Chicanos (the latter referring to Mexicans only) are already mixed-race. With the late 1900s explosion of Latino migration to the United States, there will be more mixing and thus more biracial children who have one Latino parent and one of another racial group.

American Indians and Whites

The history of American Indians and whites is full of conflict, bloodshed—and interracial mixing. As westward expansion occurred, Indians became known across the country for harboring white male sojourners who were often set up with their own huts and given Indian women as wives or servants (Johnston, p. 271). White men living with Indian women became so common they were given a title: "squaw men." Their biracial children, being bilingual and bicultural, played important frontier roles as interpreters and traders (Nabokov, p. 69).

As fighting over land increased, intermarriage became less common and more scorned among whites. Indians were portrayed as savages, and any social interaction, especially on the level of sexual intimacy, was perceived as treachery.

After the Native Americans were subdued, the U.S. government had to figure out what to do with those who had survived the decimation. The Dawes Act of 1887 gave each Indian family 160 acres of land within a reservation. Single men and women received 80 acres each. The act encouraged intermarriage: now there were white men who wanted to marry Indian women for their land (one of the unfortunate facts of miscegenation history—not all intermarriage was honorable).

If a tribe wasn't large enough to use all of the allotted acreage, it became the government's to sell to whites. This too put whites and Native Americans in closer proximity, so that mixing could occur.

The 1910 census reported that only 56.5 percent of American Indians were full-blooded Indians. By 1930 that figure had dropped to 46.3 percent (Root,

Racially Mixed People, p. 116). Some tribes remained secluded, but overall Native Americans were becoming more multiracial. Will Rogers and Vice President Charles Curtis (in office from 1928 to 1933) are two well-known Americans of Indian-white heritage.

"Black Indians"

Threatened by the thought that blacks and Indians might unite against them, whites worked to divide and conquer. For example, they offered Indians one hundred pounds for a returned slave and fifty pounds for a scalped slave. Whole Indian tribes were taken out so that escaped blacks would be unable to find refuge in their villages.

In spite of this, many blacks and Indians formed alliances, intermarried and bore children. Besides having a common enemy, they shared some cultural values, such as their views of community, nature and property ownership. By the late 1800s the Nineteenth Annual Report of the Bureau of American Ethnology reported that "a considerable proportion of the blood of the Southern Negroes (of the U.S.) is unquestionably Indian" (*Journal of Ethnic Studies,* p. 17).

In 1834 a special census was taken of the Choctaw Indians. Surveying the results, one can see how much mixture with blacks was occurring:

Jacob O'Rare, a mulatto, half Indian and half Negro . . .
James Blue, a Negro-Indian man, has an Indian wife . . .
William Lightfoot, a mulatto, half Indian and half Negro . . .
Jim Tom, half breed Negro, has an Indian wife . . .
Jacob Daniel, has a half Indian and half Negro for a wife . . .
(*Journal of Ethnic Studies,* p. 30)

There are many examples of historically significant "black Indians." Crispus Attucks, who confronted British invaders and was the first killed in the Boston Massacre inciting the American Revolution, was a runaway slave of black-Indian heritage.

Jean Baptiste Pointe du Sable was a black Indian by choice. The son of an African slave mother and a French mariner father, he came to America from Haiti. He lived with the Illinois Indians, learned their language and married an Indian woman. He, his wife and their multiracial son built the first trading post and house that eventually became the city of Chicago.

A famous black man who mixed with Indian women under some very unusual circumstances was York, slave of the explorer William Clark. He was an incredible linguist who gained much prestige among the Indians they met in their travels. York reminded the Indians of a buffalo or bear (animals they saw as powerful), so they gave him their women because they believed that power could be transmitted sexually; when they had intercourse with their wives again, York's powers would become theirs. More likely what they got out of the deal was mixed-race children.

Triracial Isolates

In some areas on the East Coast and in the South, whole groups developed which could not be classified as belonging to a single race. They formed their own isolated communities. Because these people are thought to be a mixture of black, white and Indian, social scientists often refer to them as *triracial isolates*.

After interviewing and observing many of these people in the 1950s, Brewton Berry said that though their origins were mostly obscured, their mixed-race background could be verified in their faces. He discovered some two hundred such communities, ranging in size from the thirty thousand Lumbees of North Carolina to small bands of a few families (Berry, p. 16).

The Lumbees of North Carolina date back to before the 1730s, when the first English and Scotch settlers arrived in the region of Robeson County and found a community of mixed-race folks already there. "They lived in houses, cultivated crops, spoke an English dialect, and had the manners and customs of the frontier. In a document written in the year 1754, no mention is made of Indians living in the territory, but it is said that 'a mixt Crew, a lawless People, possess the Lands without patent or paying quit rents; shot a surveyor for coming to view vacant lands being enclosed in swamps' " (Berry, p. 153). Apparently the Lumbees liked their privacy. And their presence confirms again that mixing was going on long before the American Revolution.

Black and White

The mixed-race group that has historically gotten the most attention in the United States, in spite of its relatively small size, is the direct offspring of blacks and whites. This is primarily due to the legacy of slavery, as well as obsession with racial (primarily color) differences. Although the hostility between American Indians and whites has existed as long as the hostility between blacks and whites, whites have romanticized Indians but dehumanized blacks, so that black-white mixing is considered much more abhorrent.

Mixing between black and white, however, goes back to the earliest stages of this country's development. Tens of thousands of Anglos came as indentured oorvants to pay their passage across the Atlantic. For almost one hundred years in the seventeenth century, whites were the principal source of labor in the colonies (Harris, p. 83). Interracial relations between English and African indentured servants (the latter over time being forced into race-based slavery) are considered the source of the earliest black-white mixed-race people in the United States (Williamson, p. 7).

Scientist Benjamin Banneker (born in 1731) descended from such a union. His white maternal grandmother was an Englishwoman who came to Maryland as an indentured servant. After seven years she was released and married a black slave, the son of an African king, whom she bought and freed (Johnston, p. 189). He was called Banna Ka—later changed to Bannaky, then Banneker. Banneker, sounding like a man descended from hostile races, once lamented, "Ah, why will men forget that they are brethren?"

As the colonies became established, fears of the growth of a mixed race intensified, leading to a backlash of laws and punishments intended to curb miscegenation. One of the earliest examples is from Virginia in 1630, when it was ordered "that Hugh Davis [a white man] be soundly whipped before an assemblage of Negroes and others for abusing himself to the dishonor of God and the shame of Christians by defiling his body in lying with a Negro, which fault he is to acknowledge next Sabboth day" (Johnston, p. 166).

In 1662 in Virginia, a legislative act declared that mulatto children of slave mothers would be slaves. This broke from the English tradition that children inherited the status of the father. The supposed intent of the law was to inhibit interracial sexual relations, but it conveniently supported the increase of the slave population each time a white man impregnated one of his slaves. In this same act, fornication with a black person received double the penalty of that with a white person; the clear message was that "sexual intercourse by a Christian with a black person was twice as evil as sexual intercourse with a white person" (Williamson, p. 8).

God has given us certain commands regarding sexual relations for our own welfare, but race *in and of itself* is nowhere mentioned in the Bible as a factor prohibiting sex. The Christians meting out these punishments in the American colonies were the ones who deserved a sound rebuke—for their sin of racism.

The status of biracial children born to white mothers was more problematic. In 1691 the Virginia assembly attacked black-white offspring of white women as "that abominable mixture and spurious issue." Any Englishwoman who gave birth to a black man's baby was penalized with a heavy fine or five years' servitude, and her child was made a servant until his or her thirtieth birthday. If the couple got married, they were banished from the colony (Williamson, p. 8). Other penalties to curb intermarriage included jail time and fines imposed on ministers who performed ceremonies. Portions of these fines were paid to informers.

One prominent example of mixed marriage between a black man and white woman is found in the will of John Fenwick, Lord Proprietor of New Jersey, in which he repudiates the "sin" of his granddaughter. "Item, I do except against Elizabeth Adams of having any ye leaste part of my estate, unless the Lord open her eyes to see her abominable transgression against him, me and her good father, by giving her true repentance, and forsaking ye Black ye hath been ye ruin of her, and becoming penetent [sic] of her sins; upon ye condition only I do will and require my executors to settle five hundred acres of land upon her" (Johnston, pp. 181-82). Adams apparently did not repent, for her marriage became the start of a mixed-race settlement known as Gouldtown, New Jersey.

In spite of laws and ubiquitous religious rhetoric against miscegenation, intermixing had become so common by the end of the colonial period that runaway slaves were occasionally described as being indistinguishable from whites (Johnston, p. 191). Though there were some relations between black men and white women and even some marriages going both ways, most of this mixing was undoubtedly nonmarital and nonconsensual—between white men, who had power and access, and black women (Myrdal, p. 125). President Thomas Jefferson declared that interracial sex and racially mixed offspring would "rupture the borders of caste" and "dangerously blur the division between white and black," upsetting the social order (Takaki, p. 75). Apparently his relationship with Sally Hemmings didn't count.

Both Frederick Douglass (born in 1817) and Booker T. Washington (born circa 1856) had white fathers and black mothers. They did not have relationships with their fathers, however, and both planted themselves squarely within the black race. When Douglass married a white woman in 1884, many blacks were shocked and dismayed at what they considered a traitorous act.

In the late nineteenth century, interracial social groups and networks began to form. In these contexts interracial couples and biracial people were encouraged to affirm both heritages. These forerunners to current groups such as I-Pride and Hapa Issues Forum included the Manasseh Societies (named after Joseph's half-Egyptian son) of Milwaukee and Chicago from 1892 to 1932; the Penguin Club in New York during the 1930s; the Miscegenation Club in Los Angeles; and groups in Washington, D.C., and Detroit during the 1940s (Root,

Racially Mixed People, p. 335).

Asian Americans

Asian-white and Asian American-white unions make up the largest proportion of all interracial marriages (Root, *Racially Mixed People*, p. 38). Mixed-race Asian Americans began appearing soon after the first Asians arrived in the United States.

Chinese. The Chinese were the first Asian group to come to this country. Arriving mainly between 1850 and 1882 were mostly young men hoping to make money and return to their homeland. Anti-Chinese sentiment led to the Chinese Exclusion Act of 1882, which forbade immigration until 1943; consequently the Chinese population decreased from 107,488 in 1890 to 61,639 in 1920. There was an abnormally high male-female ratio among the Chinese at this time, a condition that generally results in higher rates of intermarriage.

The first Chinese man in the United States, Yung Wing, came in 1847. He graduated from Yale and eventually married Mary Louisa Kellogg, a white woman, in 1875. Wing was a diplomat with ties to the Chinese emperor. He was highly educated and held a prominent position in the Chinese government. In spite of these things, New Englanders looked down on his marriage. Wing also became highly suspect in China. His conversion to Christianity didn't help.

The Chinese were considered a threat to racial purity just as blacks were. One man declared to the 1878 California Constitutional Convention, "Were the Chinese to amalgamate at all with our people, it would be the lowest, most vile and degraded of our race, and the result of that amalgamation would be a hybrid of the most despicable, a mongrel of the most detestable that has ever afflicted the earth." The Chinese were compared to Native Americans, and many thought they should also be put on reservations (Takaki, p. 205).

With the civil rights movement and the Immigration Act of 1965—which gave preference to newcomers with money, education and skills—negative images of the Chinese (and other Asian groups) moderated or became positive. They were seen as educated, hardworking, mannered, family-oriented and prosperous. This change favored intermarriage, particularly with whites.

Japanese. The largest wave of Japanese immigration started around 1890 and continued until 1924, when restrictive legislation was passed against them. Less than twenty years later, during World War II, over 115,000 Japanese Americans were imprisoned in concentration camps because the government had concluded that they posed a threat to national security (though Italian Americans did not, and German Americans, though scrutinized, were spared the humiliation of internment).

These prisons housed at least fourteen hundred intermarried Japanese Americans, a few of their spouses, and at least seven hundred people of mixed-race ancestry. Government officials showed discomfort with the incarceration of these families, for the nefarious reason that they did not want biracial children to be tainted by such "concentrated" contact with the suspect Japanese (Spickard, p. 53). Decisions regarding which individuals to release were based primarily on racial attributes, again proving our country's obsession with appearance, the higher value put on white-looking people, and the prevalence of the belief that how one looks determines one's belief system, loyalties, intelligence, morality and other character traits.

In Los Angeles in 1979, Japanese Americans had a higher intermarriage rate than Chinese and Koreans. Japanese were marrying out at a rate of 60.6 percent; Chinese 41.2 percent; Koreans 27.6 percent (Kitano et al., pp. 179-90). Nationally, Japanese Americans continue to have the highest outmarriage rate, leading some to wonder what will happen to Japanese culture in the United States if the rapid rate of intermixing continues.

Filipinos. A large swell of Filipino migration between 1925 and 1934 produced a gender ratio of twenty-five males to one female. (Restrictive legislation in 1934 limited immigration to fifty Filipinos a year.) As a result, 92 percent of married men married out of their group.

Filipino-white marriages had already been put to the test in California by an 1880 law that prohibited "intermarriage of white persons with Mongolians, negroes, mulattoes, or persons of mixed blood descended from a Chinaman or negro from the third generation, inclusive" (Chan, p. 60). Most Asians were unaffected by the law because they had no desire to marry whites, but Filipinos, many of whom were mixed race (primarily of Polynesian, Spanish and Chinese backgrounds), were more disconcerted. Some county clerks issued Filipinos licenses for interracial marriages since their racial classification was murky. Others wouldn't.

In 1921 Los Angeles officials decided to recognize Filipino-white marriages because Filipinos weren't "Mongolians." California's attorney general eventually sued Los Angeles County to stop its encouragement of miscegenation. Filipinos filed counter cases, and four of them reached the county superior court in 1931. In 1933 the appellate court decided for Filipinos, based on the works of nineteenth-century ethnologists that distinguished Malays ("brown") from Mongolians ("yellow"). Filipinos, the court decided, were Malays. Malays and Mongolians were *not* the same. Therefore the Filipinos were exempt from the law.

Antimiscegenation forces fought back by going to the state legislature, which unanimously passed bills to ban Filipino-white marriages again. Finally California's antimiscegenation statutes were declared unconstitutional in 1948.

Koreans. Some ten thousand Koreans immigrated to the United States in an initial wave, mainly between 1902 and 1905. Further migration ceased after the Japanese takeover of Korea (formal annexation occurred in 1910) and didn't resume until after World War II. After the Korean War (1950-1953), immigration rapidly increased. The U.S. Korean population grew from about 70,000 in 1970 to over 350,000 in 1980.

Though intermarriage occurs in the Korean American community, its out-marriage rate lags behind that of other Asian groups, most likely because Korean immigration is still relatively new. Studies have shown that in cases of immigration, intermarriage increases with each succeeding generation as people acculturate.

Koreans also exhibit fierce ethnic pride and exclusivity, at least in part due to the forced assimilation they experienced under Japanese rule. This also limits intermarriage. The exception has been in Hawaii, where in 1980, 83 percent of Korean marriages were intermarriages. (Hawaii, however, is anomalous in U.S. history. It is the one state where race mixing is not seen as strange or threatening but as normative.)

All kinds of mixes. Increased interracial marriage in the Asian American community has given rise to many multiracial people. These *hapas* are not only Asian and white but combinations of Asian and every other race, as well as mixtures of two or more Asian groups. These latter folks may experience as much tension as any biracial person, given cultural differences and historical animosities, like those between Japanese and Koreans.

Another less-publicized mixture is Asian-Native American, especially prominent in California (Root, *Racially Mixed People,* p. 122). Also to be found in California are the offspring of Punjabi Indian men who migrated before World War II and married Mexican women (Chan, p. 59).

There are many Asian-black hapas who are proud to bear the features and enjoy the cultures of both ethnic groups. Though there are examples of Asians and blacks being hostile toward one another in the United States, not all hapas of this mix feel torn between their two sides.[3]

Children of American servicemen and Vietnamese women have been the

---

[3]See "Chopsticks and Chitlins: The Afro-Asian Experience" in *Mavin,* Fall 1999, for example.

center of much controversy in the years since the Vietnam War. These children were scorned in Vietnam, where most of them remained, and the United States ignored their plight for years. Even though Congress passed an Amerasian Immigration Act in 1982 to enable children with American fathers to immigrate, it applied to those in Korea, Thailand, the Philippines and elsewhere, but not Vietnam (purportedly due to a lack of diplomatic relations between the two countries.) In 1987 the United States finally passed an Amerasian Homecoming Act for Vietnamese biracial children born between 1962 and 1976. They could immigrate with certain family members as long as they applied for visas before March 1990 (Chan, p. 163).

Latinos

"Today, the great majority of Latin Americans are what we in the United States would call 'mixed-race,' predominantly of Native American, European, and African ancestry" (Root, *Racially Mixed People*, p. 126). As in the United States, race mixing in Latin America has been around for a long time. Unfortunately, much of that mixture derives from unjust sources—colonization and slavery. Many are angry about the history of European infiltration in Latin American countries. Others have bought into racist caste systems parallel to the one in the United States, where lighter skin and European heritage is exalted and darker skin and indigenous heritage is stigmatized. Discrimination against darker and indigenous people, including mixed-race people, has left a disproportionate number of them in poverty.

Racism in Latin America is similar to that in the United States. Race mixing, however, is viewed quite differently, mainly because it is ubiquitous. "People of mixed racial ancestry came to form a much greater proportion of the population in Latin American than in Anglo America. This simple fact meant that, in varying degrees, race was neutralized as a significant social issue (or at least transformed into a class issue) throughout much of Latin America while it remains one of the most salient features of North American life" (Root, *Racially Mixed People,* p. 139).

The majority of Latinos in the United States today are Mexican Americans. By the middle of the eighteenth century in Mexico, African and part-African people constituted the second largest ethnic group. Only Native Americans were more populous. By 1900, however, mestizos (mixed-race people) had their own ethnic identity and outnumbered all other groups (Root, *Racially Mixed People,* p. 129).

From 1970 to 1992, Latinos in the United States increased from 9 million to 22.3 million—almost three times the growth rate for the population as a whole

(*Two Nations*, p. 6). The 2000 Census counted 35.5 million Hispanics. This figure represented a 60 percent increase from 1990 and was roughly equal to the number of black Americans for the first time in U.S. history.

Most likely they will follow the usual pattern of immigrants—higher intermarriage rates with each successive generation. In a recent discussion of biracial people that I led, five out of nine were of Latino and white parentage. It's a trend that will undoubtedly continue.

Not Alone

No matter where your roots lie—Asia, Africa, Europe or the Americas—if you do some research, you will almost certainly find historical examples of multiracial people with backgrounds like yours who can be meaningful to you. For example, it was significant for me to learn while doing research for this appendix that my home state of Washington owes its existence to a black-white man named George Bush (no relation to U.S. presidents—at least not *thought* to be). Someone biracial like me was responsible for the founding of the state where I was born and raised.

In the context of history, we find that we truly are not alone.

Appendix 3

Resources

Note: While I have seen or read many of the following, I have not reviewed them *all*. Please research them on the Web or in a bookstore, or contact the publishing company for more information, before buying.

Websites
Resources and Community
Bi-Racial Identity
www.geocities.com/Athens/Oracle/1103/
A site created for a sociology of education class at Columbia University. Contains statistics related to biracial births and interracial marriages; testimonies of multiracial people; the Bill of Rights for Racially Mixed People; pros and cons of a multiracial category on the census.

Center for the Study of Biracial Children
www.csbc.cncfamily.com
Created in 1991, this center located in Denver provides information, support and advocacy for interracial parents. Also seeks to serve teachers/educators and graduate students doing research. Executive director Francis Wardle can be reached at (303) 690-9008 or sicnarf@csbc.cncfamily.com.

Center for the Study of White American Culture
www.euroamerican.org
An organization that encourages dialogue among all racial and cultural groups concerning the role of white American culture in the larger American society. Operates on the premise that knowledge of one's own racial background and culture is essential for learning how to relate to people of other racial and cultural groups.

Ethnic-America On-Line
www.ethnic-america.com/eaol
A portal to ethnic-related online sites and materials; there are directories for multiple ethnic groups including "multiracial" and "multi-cultural."

The Hapa Handbook
www.hooked.net/~hapa/text/hapahandbook.html
Creator Greg Mayeda doesn't promise "everything you ever wanted to know about hapas and mixed-race people," but simply a starting point. Contains a glossary of terms and buzzwords, statistics, books and publications, documentaries, organizations, Internet resources and "High Profile Hapas."

INTERracialWeb.com
www.interracialweb.com/bin/subscribe.cgi
A directory of interracial/intercultural resources on the Web. Subscribe here and keep informed of new additions to the directory.

Iranian Mixed-Race Families
www.farsinet.com/shoharkhaleh
This site is titled "For foreign husbands of Iranian women," but any family with a Persian blend could probably find something here.

Multicultural Pavilion
http://curry.edschool.virginia.edu/go/multicultural
Created by Paul Gorski at the University of Maryland, this site has resources for teachers and diversity-awareness facilitators, activities, book and article reviews, a photo gallery and links.

My Shoes
www.myshoes.com
A place for multiracial children, adolescents and adults who have a white appearance to share their experiences.

Our Blended Family
http://go.to/interracialblend
One interracial family's website; the "Misc" page contains links to articles.

A Place for Us (APFU)
www.angelfire.com/nv/aplaceforus
An organization committed to supporting and encouraging those involved in interracial relationships and their families.

Secret Daughter
www.pbs.org/wgbh/pages/frontline/shows/secret/
The story of a mixed-race daughter and the mother who gave her away. Includes portraits of multiracial Americans, how to research your family history and information about the multiracial heritage of famous families.

Spanish/English Bilingual Families
http://pages.ivillage.com/bilingual
Resources and opportunities to interact with others.

Students of Mixed Heritage and Culture
www.amherst.edu/~smhac/links/mlinks.html
A thorough listing of resources compiled for Pearl Fuyo Gaskins's book *What Are You?* is on this Amherst student group's website.

"You Don't Look Japanese!"
www.angelfire.com/or/biracial
A compilation of resources, including many for Asian mixed-race people.

News and Issues
The Multiracial Activist
www.multiracial.com
Covers social and civil liberties issues of interest to multiracial people, interracial families and transracial adoptees. Includes an extensive links directory with multiple multiracial and multicultural websites and chat rooms.

http://racerelations.about.com/newsissues
News and articles related to race and culture, including multiracial and interracial issues.

Articles
"All Mixed Up"
www.salon.com/news/feature/2000/02/14/mixed_race/index.html
Salon.com features a series of articles on America's multiracial future.

"Blurring the Lines"
www.washington.edu/alumni/columns/dec96
Maria P. P. Root, a clinical psychologist who has edited groundbreaking books on the multiracial experience, is featured.

"The Identity Development of Multiracial Youth"
http://eric-web.tc.columbia.edu/digests/dig137
This article, from the Clearinghouse on Urban Education at the Teachers College of Columbia University, calls educators to be aware of the growing population of multiracial children and to encourage their identity development.

"Multiracial Families"
www.counseling.org/conference/advocacy6.htm
This article calls on counselors to understand the experiences of multiracial individuals and families for the sake of more effective counseling. Contains a good list of resources at the end: books, children's books, websites, and a list of organizations for interracial families and multiracial people by state.

Advocacy Groups
Association of Multi-Ethnic Americans (AMEA)
ameapres@aol.com
www.ameasite.org

Hapa Issues Forum
www.hapaissuesforum.org

Project RACE—Reclassify All Children Equally
ProjRACE@aol.com
www.projectrace.com

College Groups
Check the website of *Mavin* magazine (www.mavin.net) for a list of such organizations in North America.

Interracial Family Organizations
Contact AMEA for a group near you. Here is a sampling from around the nation.

Biracial Family Network
P.O. Box 3214
Chicago, IL 60654
Bfnnewsltr@aol.com

GIFT (Getting Interracial/Intercultural Families Together)
P.O. Box 1281
Montclair, NJ 07042
NJGIFT@aol.com
http://members.aol.com/njgift/index.html

Honor Our New Ethnic Youth (HONEY)
P.O. Box 23241
Eugene, OR 97402

Interracial Club of Buffalo
P.O. Box 400 Amherst Branch
Buffalo, NY 14226
716-875-6958

Interracial Family and Social Alliance
P.O. Box 35109
Dallas, TX 75235-0109
www.flash.net/~mata9/ifsa.htm

Interracial Family Circle
P.O. Box 53291
Washington, DC 20009
Ifcweb@hotmail.com
www.geocities.com/Heartland/Estates/4496

Interracial Family Network
Family Enhancement Center
2120 Fordem Avenue
Madison, WI 53704
608-241-5150

Interracial Family Network of Seattle-King County
16541 Redmond Way, Suite 105
Redmond, WA 98052-4482
www.isomedia.com/homes/duncan/interracial.html

Interracial-Intercultural Pride (I-Pride)
P.O. Box 11811
Berkeley, CA 94712-11811
www.ameasite.org

Multicultural Families Group of Tallahassee, Florida
multiculturalTal@netscape.net
http://sites.netscape.net/multiculturalTal

Multiracial Americans of Southern California (MASC)
12228 Venice Boulevard, Suite 452
Los Angeles, CA 90066
www.multiculti.org

Multiracial Family Circle
Kansas City, MO
www.cdiversity.com/mfc

Multiracial Families Program
Hiawatha Branch YMCA
4100 28th Avenue South
Minneapolis, MN 55406
www.primenet.com/~dsmyre/mac.htm

Specifically for Parents
Businesses and Organizations
FamilyCulture.com
www.familyculture.com/familyculture/articles.htm
Contains a number of articles related to raising mixed-race children. FamilyCulture.com
provides educational and cultural resources for diverse families and their service
providers, with a special focus on Asian and multicultural families.

Great Owl Books
www.viconet.com/~greatowlbooks
A family-owned business that specializes in providing books for interracial families.

InterracialFamily.com
www.interracialfamily.com
Self-described as a positive and supportive presence for interracial/intercultural couples and families.

Lee and Low Books
www.leeandlow.com
Publisher of multicultural children's books.

Books and Magazines
Raising Black and Biracial Children Magazine
P.O. Box 17479
Beverly Hills, CA 90209
http://members.aol.com/intrace/index.html

Wardle, Francis. *Tomorrow's Children.* Available only from the Center for the Study of Biracial Children: www.csbc.cncfamily.com

Wright, Marguerite. *I'm Chocolate, You're Vanilla: Raising Healthy Black and Biracial Children in a Race-Conscious World.* San Francisco: Jossey-Bass, 1998.

Transracial Adoption Resources
Adopt
www.adopting.org/inter.html
This website provides assistance, information and support for adoptive families. The address above leads directly to an article titled "Interracial Families."

Asian Adult Adoptees of Washington
4756 University Place, NE, Suite 224
Seattle, WA 98105
aaaw@u.washington.edu
www.deestudios.com/aaaw/
Created in 1997, AAAW has the mission of creating a foundation of emotional, social and economic support that allows crosscultural adoptees the ability to exist and grow in their current surroundings.

Interracial Adoption
ww2.netnitco.net/users/tank/adopt3.htm
Resources and opportunities to interact with other families that are interracial by adoption.

Korean-American Adoptee Adoptive Family Network (KAAN)
P.O. Box 5585
El Dorado Hills, CA 95762
916-933-1447
KAANet@aol.com

National Adoption Information Clearinghouse
www.calib.com/naic/pubs/s_trans.htm
A national resource for information on all aspects of adoption for professionals, pol-
icymakers and the general public. The address leads directly to information about
transracial adoption.

PACT—An Adoption Alliance
3450 Sacramento Street, Suite 239
San Francisco, CA 94110
Info@pactadopt.org
www.pactadopt.org
This website's goal is to maintain the Internet's most comprehensive site addressing
issues for adopted children of color. It offers articles, profiles of families, links, a
book reference guide and opportunities to interact with others. PACT is a national
nonprofit organization seeking to educate birth families and adoptive families on
matters of race and adoption.

Voices from the Borderlands
www.ibar.com/borderlands
A site seeking submissions from transracial adoptees about their experience.

Magazines
Mavin: The Mixed Race Experience
600 First Ave., Suite 501
Seattle, WA 98104-2229
888-77-MAVIN
www.mavin.net

InterRace
P.O. Box 17479
Beverly Hills, CA 90209
http://members.aol.com/intrace/index.html

E-Zines
Interracial Voice
P.O. Box 560185
College Point, NY 11356-0185
Intvoice@webcom.com
www.webcom.com/~intvoice

Métisse Magazine Online: The Magazine for Today's Multiracial and Multicultural
Woman
www.metisse.com

Documentaries
Films are expensive to buy and often even to rent. Check with your local library or

social services programs to see if they have a copy. Also see <www.lib.berkeley.edu/ MRC/mixedracevid.html> for a listing of movies about the multiracial experience.

"Are You Black, White or What?" Produced and written by Lillian Anne Paulmier. A WHYY-TV production, 1996; approximately 50 minutes. Inspired by her young biracial son and the difficult identity choices he will eventually encounter, Paulmier interviews seven biracial adults about how their experiences have affected their self-views.

WHYY (Corporation for Public Broadcasting)
150 N. 6th Street
Philadelphia, PA 19106
215-351-3308

Domino: Interracial People and the Search for Identity. Directed by Shanti Thakur. Produced by Shanti Thakur, Dennis Murphy and Silva Basmajian. National Film Board of Canada in association with Lucinda Films, Inc. Princeton, N.J.: Films for the Humanities and Sciences, 1995; 45 minutes.

Contact Filmakers Library for the next six films:
124 E. 40th Street, Suite 901
New York, NY 10016
212-808-4980
info@filmakers.com
www.filmakers.com

Between Black and White. Produced by Giannella Garrett. Independently produced, 1994; 26 minutes. Four people, including Danzy Senna, author of *Caucasia,* talk about having mixed-race heritage. Video's homepage: www.catchafire.com/reelrep/bbw.

Just Black? Multiracial Identity. Produced by Francine Winddance Twine, Jonathan F. Warren and Francisco Ferrandiz Martin. Independently produced, 1992; 57 minutes. Several college students who have some black ancestry are interviewed about their experiences establishing a racial identity.

None of the Above: People of Multiracial Heritage. Directed by Erika Surat Andersen. University of Southern California, 1994; 23 minutes. Based on the filmmaker's own search for identity and community as a person of Asian Indian and Danish descent, this is an inside look at the emotional reality of being racially unclassifiable in a society obsessed with racial categories.

Seoul II Soul. Directed by Hak J. Chung. University of Southern California, School of Cinema and Television, 1999; 25 minutes. An African American veteran of the Korean War and his Korean wife open their home so we can learn about their interracial family, including three grown children.

Struggle for Identity: Issues in Transracial Adoption. Directed by David Gluck. Produced by Photosynthesis Productions, 2000; 20 minutes. This video brings into focus the issues of race, culture and identity in adoptive or foster families. Teens speak candidly about their conflicts and confusions.

Suzanne Bonnar; The Blackburg Connection. A Garrison Kennedy Production for BBC Scotland, 1997; 29 minutes. The story of a mixed-race child growing up in Scotland who seeks out her African American father.

Books
Adult Fiction
Brown, Rosellen. *Half a Heart.* New York: Farrar, Straus & Giroux, 2000.
Budhos, Marina. *House of Waiting.* New York: Global City Press, 1995.
Dorris, Michael. *A Yellow Raft in Blue Water.* New York: Henry Holt, 1987.
Jacobs, Rayda. *The Middle Children.* Toronto: Second Story, 1994.
Senna, Danzy. *Caucasia.* New York: Riverhead Books, 1998.
Smith, Zadie. *White Teeth.* New York: Vintage Books, 2000.
Tyau, Kathleen. *A Little Too Much Is Enough.* New York: Farrar, Straus & Giroux, 1995.
West, Dorothy. *The Wedding.* New York: Doubleday, 1995.

Adolescent and Young Adult Fiction
Dorris, Michael. *The Window.* New York: Hyperion, 1997.
Fenkl, Heinz Insu. *Memories of My Ghost Brother.* New York: Dutton, 1996.
Flake, Sharon. *The Skin I'm In.* New York: Jump at the Sun/Hyperion, 1998.
Garland, Sherry. *The Last Rainmaker.* San Diego: Harcourt Brace, 1997.
————. *Song of the Buffalo Boy.* San Diego: Harcourt Brace Jovanovich, 1992.
Hamilton, Virginia. *Arilla Sun Down.* New York: Greenwillow Books, 1976.
Meyer, Carolyn. *Jubillee Journey.* San Diego: Harcourt Brace, 1997.
O'Connor, Barbara. *Me and Rupert Goody.* New York: Frances Foster Books/Farrar, Straus & Giroux, 1999.
Pullman, Philip. *The Broken Bridge.* New York: Alfred A. Knopf, 1990.
Viglucci, Pat Costa. *Sun Dance at Turtle Rock.* Rochester, N.Y.: Stone Pine/Patri, 1996.

Children's
Adoff, Arnold. *All the Colors of the Race: Poems.* New York: Lothrop, Lee & Shepard, 1982.
————. *Black Is Brown Is Tan.* New York: Harper & Row, 1973.
Davol, Marguerite. *Black, White, Just Right!* Morton Grove, Ill.: A. Whitman, 1993.
Hamanaka, Sheila. *All the Colors of the Earth.* New York: Morrow Junior, 1994.
Igus, Toyomi. *Two Mrs. Gibsons.* San Francisco: Children's Book, 1996.
Kandel, Bethany. *Trevor's Story: Growing Up Biracial.* Minneapolis: Lerner, 1997.
Katz, Karen. *The Colors of Us.* New York: Holt Rinehart & Winston, 1999.
Kissinger, Katie. *All the Colors We Are: The Story of How We Get Our Skin Color.* St. Paul: Redleaf, 1994.

Lacapa, Kathleen. *Less Than Half, More Than Whole*. Flagstaff, Ariz.: Northland, 1994.

Mandelbaum, Pili. *You Be Me; I'll Be You*. Brooklyn, N.Y.: Kane/Miller, 1990.

McKay, Lawrence, Jr. *Journey Home*. New York: Lee & Low, 1998.

Nash, Renea D. *Everything You Need to Know About Being a Biracial/Biethnic Child*. New York: Rosen, 1995.

Senisi, Ellen B. *For My Family, Love, Allie*. Morton Grove, Ill.: Albert Whitman, 1998.

Simon, Norma. *Why Am I Different?* Chicago: Albert Whitman, 1976.

www.soemadison.wisc.edu/ccbc/public/interrac.htm

This website, published by the Cooperative Children's Book Center at the University of Wisconsin, lists books that depict interracial/multiracial/multiethnic children and families.

Essays/Interviews

Camper, Carol. *Miscegenation Blues: Voices of Mixed Race Women*. Toronto: Sister Vision, 1994.

Funderburg, Lise. *Black, White, Other: Biracial Americans Talk About Race and Identity*. New York: William Morrow, 1994.

Gaskins, Pearl Fuyo. *What Are You?* New York: Henry Holt, 1999.

Gay, Kathlyn. *"I Am Who I Am": Speaking Out About Multiracial Identity*. New York: Franklin Watts, 1995.

Gillespie, Peggy, and Gigi Kaeser. *Of Many Colors: Portraits of Multiracial Families*. Amherst: University of Massachusetts Press, 1997.

Lee, Joann Faung Jean. *Asian American Experiences in the United States*. New York: New Press, 1992. Devotes a section to interviews of Asians in interracial relationships and families.

McKelvey, Robert S. *The Dust of Life: America's Children Abandoned in Vietnam*. Seattle: University of Washington Press, 1999.

O'Hearn, Claudine Chiawei, ed. *Half + Half: Writers on Growing Up Biracial and Bicultural*. New York: Pantheon, 1998.

Penn, William S., ed. *As We Are Now: Mixblood Essays on Race and Identity*. Berkeley: University of California Press, 1997.

History/Social Science

Berry, Brewton. *Almost White*. New York: Macmillan, 1963.

Bode, Janet. *Different Worlds: Interracial and Cross-Cultural Dating*. New York: Franklin Watts, 1989.

Brown, Ursula. *The Interracial Experience: Growing Up Black/White Racially Mixed in the United States*. Westport, Conn.: Praeger, 2000.

Chan, Sucheng. *Asian Americans: An Interpretive History*. Boston: Twayne, 1991.

Chiong, Jane Ayers. *Racial Categorization of Multiracial Children in Schools*. Westport, Conn.: Bergin & Garvey, 1998.

Hacker, Andrew. *Two Nations: Black and White, Separate, Hostile, Unequal*. New York: Ballantine, 1992.

Harris, Marvin. *Patterns of Race in the Americas*. New York: W. W. Norton, 1964.

Johnston, James Hugo. *Race Relations in Virginia and Miscegenation in the South, 1776-1860*. Amherst: University of Massachusetts Press, 1970.

Katz, William Loren. *Black Indians: A Hidden Heritage*. New York: Aladdin, 1997.

Korgen, Kathleen Odell. *From Black to Biracial: Transforming Racial Identity Among Americans*. Westport, Conn.: Praeger, 1998.

Myrdal, Gunnar. *An American Dilemma*. New York: Harper & Row, 1944, 1962.

Nabokov, Peter. *Native American Testimony: A Chronicle of Indian-White Relations from Prophecy to the Present*. New York: Viking, 1991.

Nash, Gary. *Forbidden Love: The Secret History of Mixed-Race America*. New York: Henry Holt, 1999.

Root, Maria P. P. *Love's Revolution: Racial Intermarriage*. Philadelphia: Temple University Press, 2000.

———, ed. *The Multiracial Experience: Racial Borders as the New Frontier*. Thousand Oaks, Calif.: Sage, 1996.

———, ed. *Racially Mixed People in America*. Newbury Park, Calif.: Sage, 1992.

Spencer, Jon Michael. *The New Colored People: The Mixed-Race Movement in America*. New York: New York University Press, 1997.

Speth, Marcia Ann. *One Drop: History of an American Family from the "Mayflower" to the Millennium*. Los Angeles: Olive Grove, 2000.

Spickard, Paul. *Mixed Blood: Intermarriage and Ethnic Identity in Twentieth-Century America*. Madison: University of Wisconsin Press, 1989.

Stonequist, Everett V. *The Marginal Man*. New York: Russell & Russell, 1961.

Sung, Betty Lee. *Chinese American Intermarriage*. New York: Center for Migration Studies, 1990.

Takaki, Ronald. *A Different Mirror: A History of Multicultural America*. Boston: Little, Brown, 1993.

———. *Iron Cages: Race and Culture in 19th Century America*. New York: University of Oxford Press, 2000.

Williams-Leon, Teresa, and Cynthia L. Nakashima. *The Sum of Our Parts: Mixed-Heritage Asian Americans*. Philadelphia: Temple University Press, 2001.

Williamson, Joel. *New People: Miscegenation and Mulattoes in the United States*. New York: Free Press, 1980.

Yancey, George A. *Beyond Black and White: Reflections on Racial Reconciliation*. Grand Rapids, Mich.: Baker, 1996.

Zack, Naomi. *Race and Mixed Race*. Philadelphia: Temple University Press, 1993.

———, ed. *American Mixed Race: The Culture of Microdiversity*. Lanham, Md.: Rowman & Littlefield, 1995.

Memoir/Biography

Arboldea, Teja. *In the Shadow of Race: Growing Up as a Multiethnic, Multicultural and "Multiracial" American*. Mahwah, N.J.: Lawrence Erlbaum Associates, 1998.

Derricotte, Toi. *The Black Notebooks: An Interior Journey.* New York: W. W. Norton, 1997.

Haizlip, Shirlee Taylor. *The Sweeter the Juice: A Family Memoir in Black and White.* New York: Simon & Schuster, 1994.

Hall, Wade. *Passing for Black: The Life and Careers of Mae Street Kidd.* Lexington, Ky.: University Press of Kentucky, 1998.

Jacobs, Harriet A. *Incidents in the Life of a Slave Girl.* Cambridge, Mass.: Harvard University Press, 1987.

Jones, Lisa. *Bulletproof Diva: Tales of Race, Sex and Hair.* New York: Doubleday, 1994.

Lazarre, Jane. *Beyond the Whiteness of Whiteness: Memoir of a White Mother of Black Sons.* Durham, N.C.: Duke University Press, 1996.

McBride, James. *The Color of Water: A Black Man's Tribute to His White Mother.* New York: Riverhead, 1996.

Minerbrook, Scott. *Divided to the Vein: A Journey into Race and Family.* New York: Harcourt Brace, 1996.

Obama, Barack. *Dreams from My Father: A Story of Race and Inheritance.* New York: Times Books/Random House, 1995.

Page, Clarence. *Showing My Color: Impolite Essays on Race and Identity.* New York: HarperCollins, 1996.

See, Lisa. *On Gold Mountain: The One-Hundred-Year Odyssey of a Chinese-American Family.* New York: St. Martin's Press, 1995.

Walker, Rebecca. *Black, White and Jewish: Autobiography of a Shifting Self.* New York: Riverhead, 2001.

Woodley, Randy. *Mixed Blood, Not Mixed Up: Finding God-Given Identity in a Multicultural World.* Self-published, 2000. The author is Keetoowah Cherokee. To order, visit <www.eagles-wingsmin.com>, write rw@eagles-wingsmin.com or call 205-559-8100.

Transracial Adoption

Bishoff, Tonya, and Jo Rankin, eds. *Seeds from a Silent Tree: An Anthology by Korean Adoptees.* Glendale, Calif.: Pandal, 1997.

Melanson, Yvette, with Claire Safran. *Looking for Lost Bird: A Jewish Woman Discovers Her Navajo Roots.* New York: Bard/Avon, 1999.

Bibliography

Angier, Natalie. "Do Races Differ? Not Really, DNA Shows," *New York Times*, August 22, 2000 <www.nytimes.com>.

Bakke, Raymond. *A Theology As Big As The City*. Downers Grove, Ill.: InterVarsity Press, 1997.

Berry, Brewton. *Almost White*. New York: Macmillan, 1963.

Chan, Sucheng. *Asian Americans: An Interpretive History*. Boston: Twayne, 1991.

Domino: Interracial People and the Search for Identity. Directed by Shanti Thakur. Produced by Shanti Thakur, Dennis Murphy, and Silva Basmajian. Princeton, N.J.: Films for the Humanities and Sciences, 1995.

Forbes, Jack D. "Mulattoes and People of Color in Anglo-North America: Implications for Black-Indian Relations." *The Journal of Ethnic Studies*. 12, no. 2: 21.

Funderburg, Lise. *Black, White, Other: Biracial Americans Talk About Race and Identity*. New York: William Morrow, 1994.

Grant, Madison. *The Passing of the Great Race*. New York: C. Scribner's Sons, 1922.

Harris, Marvin. *Patterns of Race in the Americas*. New York: W. W. Norton, 1964.

Johnston, James Hugo. *Race Relations in Virginia and Miscegnation in the South, 1776-1860*. Amherst: University of Massachusetts Press, 1970.

Kitano, Harry H.L., Wai-Tsang Young, Lynn Chai, Herbert Hatanaka. "Asian-American Interracial Marriage." *Journal of Marriage and the Family*, February 24, 1984, pp. 179-90.

Mains, David and Karen. *Abba: How God Parents Us*. Wheaton, Ill.: Harold Shaw, 1989.

Mills, Candy, and Gabe Grosz. "Interrace Matters," *InterRace*, fall 1997: 5.

Myrdal, Gunnar. *An American Dilemma*. New York: Harper & Row, 1944, 1962.

Nabokov, Peter. *Native American Testimony: A Chronicle of Indian-White Relations from Prophecy to the Present*. New York: Viking, 1991.

O'Hearn, Claudine Chiawei, ed. *Half + Half: Writers on Growing Up Biracial and Bicultural*. New York: Pantheon, 1998.

Root, Maria. Paper presented at "Color Lines in the 21st Century: Multiracialism in a Racially Divided World." Chicago, Ill., September 1998.

Root, Maria, ed. *Racially Mixed People in America*. Newbury Park, Calif.: Sage, 1992.

Spickard, Paul. *Mixed Blood: Intermarriage and Ethnic Identity in Twentieth-Century America*. Madison, Wis.: University of Wisconsin Press, 1989.

Sung, Betty Lee. *Chinese American Intermarriage*. New York: Center for Migration Studies, 1990.

Takaki, Ronald. *A Different Mirror: A History of Multicultural America*. Boston: Little, Brown, 1993.

Tatum, Beverly Daniel. *Why Are All the Black Kids Sitting Together in the Cafeteria?* New York: BasicBooks, 1997.

Usry, Glenn, and Craig Keener. *Black Man's Religion*. Downers Grove, Ill.: InterVarsity Press, 1996.

Websters's New World Dictionary. Edited by David B. Giralnik. 2nd college ed. New York: World, 1980.

Webster's II New Riverside Dictionary. New York: Houghton Mifflin, 1984.

Williamson, Joel. *New People: Miscegnation and Mulattoes in the United States*. New York: Louisiana State University Press, 1995.

Zwingle, Erla. "National Geographic" <www.nationalgeographic.com/2000/culture/global>.